The Complete Multifaith Resource for Primary Religious Education

The Complete Multifaith Resource for Primary Religious Education Ages 7–11 is a definitive teaching and learning aid for cross-religious exploration in the classroom, offering stimulating and detailed ways in which to apply a concepts-based approach to the teaching of RE. It provides a model for learning which engages children and encourages the development of higher-order thinking skills and which can be applied to other subject areas in a cross-curricular setting.

Comprising a book and CD-ROM, *The Complete Multifaith Resource* features key concepts that underpin religious beliefs and practices and that are key to effective learning in RE for the target age level. Each concept chapter provides a wealth of material which will enable teachers to lead their pupils through the learning experience. Resources can be displayed on an interactive whiteboard for classroom viewing, or alternatively printed out for pupils to use during individual and group activities, requiring no further search for resources. This includes:

- stories, pictures and questions to prompt discussion
- writing frames, sort cards, matching pairs and other engaging activities.

This indispensable tool provides a modern, innovative and refreshing approach to teaching RE that has already proved to be effective in a large number of schools and can be applied to the effective delivery of an agreed syllabus for RE. Each chapter is introduced by looking at the key concept from a Christian point of view, and is then examined from the perspectives of the other major world faiths, including Buddhism, Judaism, Islam, Hinduism and Sikhism.

The Complete Multifaith Resource for Primary Religious Education Ages 7–11 will be of value not only to RE managers and leaders, but also to primary phase teachers who may have little confidence or expertise in teaching RE. Trainee teachers and those studying on education courses will also benefit from gaining a better understanding of the concepts-based approach to the teaching of RE as expounded by the Hampshire, Portsmouth and Southampton Agreed Syllabus.

Judith Lowndes is currently a general inspector for primary RE in Hampshire. She has extensive experience of teaching primary pupils and advising on religious education provision, and has lectured on religious education provision to students and trainee teachers in higher education. She has contributed to a number of RE books and is co-author of the recently published Fulton textbook *Primary Religious Education: A New Approach.*

Acknowledgements

Acknowledgements are due to Hampshire County Council, Hampshire SACRE and Hampshire, Portsmouth and Southampton teachers who have worked with some of the material included in this book. Any works included that were previously published by Hampshire County Council are under its copyright and are included with its permission, by licensed agreement.

Particular acknowledgements are due to Clive Erricker who is a friend and, until recently was my colleague. The conceptual enquiry approach and methodology that this book recommends is his brainchild. We worked on implementing the methodology in schools over a number of years, and the material in this book is my attempt to support teachers in applying this particular approach effectively in their classrooms.

The Complete Multifaith Resource for Primary Religious Education

Ages 7–11

Judith Lowndes

Routledge
Taylor & Francis Group

LONDON AND NEW YORK

First published 2012
by Routledge
2 Park Square, Milton Park, Abingdon, Oxon OX14 4RN

Simultaneously published in the USA and Canada
by Routledge
711 Third Avenue, New York, NY 10017

Routledge is an imprint of the Taylor & Francis Group, an informa business

British Library Cataloguing in Publication Data
A catalogue record for this book is available from the British Library

Library of Congress Cataloging in Publication Data
Lowndes, Judith.
The complete multifaith resource for primary RE : ages 7–11 / Judith Lowndes.
   p. cm.
1. Religious education of children. 2. Education, Elementary. 3. Christianity and other religions--Study and teaching (Elementary) I. Title.
   BL1475.3.L69 2011
     200.71--dc22

                                        2011011714

ISBN: 978-0-415-66868-2 (pbk)
ISBN: 978-0-203-81634-9 (ebk)

Typeset in Helvetica
by Saxon Graphics Ltd, Derby

Illustrations by Gary Holmes

MIX
Paper from
responsible sources
FSC
www.fsc.org FSC® C004839

Printed and bound in Great Britain by the MPG Books Group

Contents

Introduction

This publication provides an approach for teaching religious education which has proved to be effective in a large number of schools. It focuses on an enquiry into concepts or 'key ideas', and employs a particular cycle of learning which can be applied to a locally agreed syllabus for religious education. This book and the accompanying CD look at religious education (RE) specifically, but in the units of work teachers will see opportunities to apply the methodology to and make links with other curriculum areas. Those teachers who employ P4C (Philosophy for Children) in their classrooms will also recognise the open enquiry methods that this book promotes. This is particularly valuable for those schools seeking to develop skills across the curriculum to improve pupils' learning.

This approach was originally developed to inform the production of the agreed syllabus for RE in Hampshire, Portsmouth and Southampton, and was later adopted by Westminster's local authority. As a result it has been tried and tested by hundreds of teachers in the south of the UK with great success. Research carried out in Hampshire, Portsmouth and Southampton schools (K. Wedell, *The Living Difference Evaluation Project Report*, 2009: http://hias.hants.gov.uk/re/course/view.php?id=42) indicates that pupils and teachers are enthusiastic about this development in RE. Evidence shows that pupils' attainment in RE is improved as a result. For full exploration of this conceptual enquiry methodology read C. Erricker, J. Lowndes and E. Bellchambers, *Primary Religious Education: A New Approach* (Oxford: Routledge, 2011).

Why focus on concepts?

Religious education has a legacy of developing learning through exploring religious material such as important figures, festivals and celebrations, stories, beliefs and practices. The focus has often been on acquisition of knowledge. For example, a class of pupils may be exploring the Jewish festival of Passover. They hear the story of Moses leading the Israelites out of Egypt and act it out in the hall, they create art work for a display in the classroom illustrating the ten plagues, they explore and make Seder plates and they role play a Jewish family celebrating the Passover meal . Teacher and pupils have a great time. The emphasis, however, is on what Jews do at Passover. Although pupils might be fully engaged with the lessons, the information about Passover might have no point of resonance with pupils, and as a result, there may be limited understanding of why Jewish people would engage with such activities. Pupils may have had the further opportunity to reflect on their own family celebrations, but again, this would not lead them any closer to understanding the significance of Passover for Jews.

The approach in this book recommends that teachers should focus on one of several potential concepts or key ideas that underpin the religious material that has been selected. As children engage, in detail, with the particular concepts, they are in a position to relate to the concept themselves, make sense of the concepts within their own experience, and better analyse the significance of that concept for the religious people being explored. This conceptual enquiry methodology enables pupils to recognise and gain insight into the meaning and significance of human behaviour, both religious and non-religious.

In relation to the example of the festival of Passover, the concept of *freedom* is one of several that is significant for Jews at Passover and which can be a focus for learning in this unit of work. Using the cycle of learning that this book demonstrates, therefore, would enable pupils to enquire into the meaning of *freedom* and the breadth of interpretations and responses to that concept. Pupils would explore how Jews express the idea of *freedom* at the festival of Passover by exploring the story, the rituals, the songs, and the symbolic foods that reflect the celebration of *freedom* for Jews. They consider the value of *freedom* for Jews and why they continue to celebrate it. Pupils are then provided with opportunities to reflect on their own responses to and experiences of *freedom*, and consider how *freedom* can affect their lives and how *freedom* affects others too, in different and similar ways. A point of resonance is achieved that enables pupils to engage with and interrogate the idea of *freedom* and its effect, relate this understanding to the Jewish response to the concept, and recognise different issues that are raised as a result. This approach moves pupils far beyond basic recall of stories and religious practices, and engages them in opportunities for critical analysis and opportunities to respond with their own thoughts and ideas.

Which concepts or key ideas should we focus on?

Within Key Stage (KS) 2, teachers often engage the pupils with familiar territory and then extend their experience and understanding. With that in mind, this publication illustrates how children can enquire into some concepts that are part of common human experience. These are classified as group A concepts (see Figure 1.1). Within this category are the concepts of *community*, *freedom*, *peace*, *suffering* and *sacrifice*. There are many more potential concepts for exploring RE within this category. Many are simple, such as *remembering*, *special* and *belonging*, but these would be better approached with younger pupils in KS 1 or the Foundation Stage. Units of work for infants are developed for simple group A concepts in the partner book to this publication, *The Complete Multifaith Resource for Primary RE: Ages 4–7*.

Group B concepts are common to many religions (see Figure 1.1), such as *holy*, *worship*, *disciple* and *God*. These concepts engage pupils in figurative language, and these are more frequently introduced at KS 2. Group C concepts are those that are exclusive to each of the religious traditions, such as *dukkha*, *resurrection*, *umma*, *sewa*, *darshan* and *mitzvot*. These very specific religious concepts require a more sophisticated level of engagement and interpretation, and are often considered to be more appropriate for KS 3 and 4 students, so they have not been included in this publication.

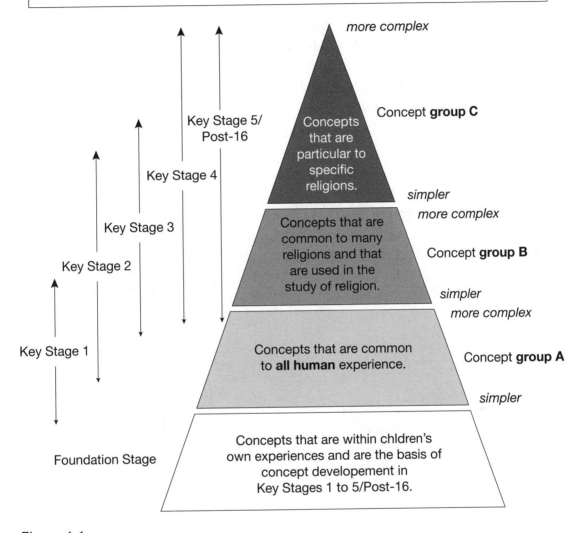

Hierarchy of concepts

This diagram illustrates how concepts can be applied within the key stages.

☐ = Group A concepts are concepts that are common to all human experience.

■ = Group B concepts are concepts shared by many religions and are used in the study of religion.

■ = Group C concepts are concepts specific to particular religions.

more complex

Key Stage 5/ Post-16

Key Stage 4

Key Stage 3

Key Stage 2

Key Stage 1

Foundation Stage

Concepts that are particular to specific religions.

Concept **group C**

simpler
more complex

Concepts that are common to many religions and that are used in the study of religion.

Concept **group B**

simpler
more complex

Concepts that are common to **all human** experience.

Concept **group A**

simpler

Concepts that are within chldren's own experiences and are the basis of concept developement in Key Stages 1 to 5/Post-16.

Figure 1.1

What is the cycle of learning for?

The cycle of learning is a particular methodology which provides a structure which enables children to focus on and enquire into a concept. Teachers will recognise some of the strategies and techniques employed within the cycle that can make a strong contribution to developing thinking skills. The methodology engages children in thinking beyond basic recall, and encourages children to engage with and develop higher-order skills such as reflection, speculation, categorization, application, evaluation and analysis. The methodology enables pupils to grow in their understanding of concepts, and recognise their significance within their own experience and the experience of religious people. This approach to RE is to enable children to *interpret religion in relation to human experience*. Those teachers who work with an agreed syllabus that requires pupils to *learn about religion* and to *learn from religion*, find that this methodology provides a meaningful focus and link between the two attainment targets

How does the cycle of learning work?

Figure 1.2 illustrates how the methodology works and the purpose of each element of the cycle of learning. Readers will find this diagram at the start of each unit of work demonstrating some key questions for each element of the cycle in relation to the identified concept. Note that there are two potential starting places: Communicate or Apply. The starting place for each unit of work in this book is indicated by "Step 1" and the learning follows the sequence around the cycle.

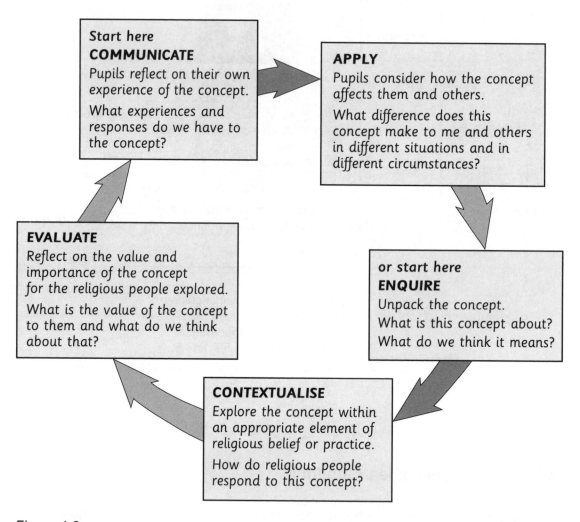

Figure 1.2

Communicate

When the concept is one drawn from group A, and pupils are in a position to talk about, share and reflect on their own experience of the concept, this is a useful place to start. Teachers will often want to provide a stimulus with which pupils can identify, and this will engage their thinking and promote discussions. There will often be a reinforcement activity here such as circle time, art and craftwork, drawing and annotating or perhaps drama or role play.

Apply

This section is closely linked to and develops out of **communicate**. In this section the teacher should challenge the pupils to think beyond their initial responses. How does the concept affect them in their lives? Does everyone think the same way about this concept? Does everyone have the same experience? Will they always feel like this about the concept? Do they think they might feel the same in different circumstances? Paired talking, group discussion and the P4C community of enquiry work well here, and so does role play.

Enquire

In this section the teacher leads the children to explore a broader interpretation of the concept. For example pupils will have been able to share their own experiences of a concept (within **communicate**), and here, the teacher could provide examples of the concept to enable pupils to explore and consider its particular characteristics. For some concepts this may be the ideal starting point. If the concept is in group B (one that is common to many religions), it will be less familiar to pupils and may require some stimuli or examples to illustrate the meaning. Brainstorming, concept mapping, sorting and categorising words, listing features, hypothesising and speculating about possible definitions, group and class speaking and listening within a community of enquiry are useful techniques for this section.

Contextualise

Here the teacher draws on religious material to illustrate how people of that faith respond to the concept. Teachers find this focus on selected aspects of a religion liberating and very worthwhile. It is particularly important in this part of the cycle to keep the concept at the centre of learning. It is not acquisition of knowledge that is important here, but fundamentally that pupils recognise the importance of the concept to the religious people. In this **contextualise** section pupils can be involved in visits, speaking to visitors, art and craft work, cooking, music, dance, drama and so on. This element also provides opportunities for personal research and developing information and communication technology (ICT) skills.

Evaluate

This section emanates from and is very closely linked to **contextualise**. Here pupils are encouraged to reflect on why the concept is important to those people who have just been investigated, and what difference it makes to their lives. Pupils should also consider and express their own views about the significance of the concept to the religious people being studied. Visitors are particularly valuable, but if this is not possible, email correspondents could be organised. Discussion, role play, hot seating, completing speech bubbles and class debates are helpful strategies to employ within this section.

How to use this publication effectively

In this book you will find the concept-led enquiry approach applied to five different concepts (**community**, **God**, **holy**, **symbol** and **ritual**). They are all contextualised within aspects of Christianity which all teachers should find useful, as it is a legal requirement that Christianity is taught in all key stages. There are also examples of material from the other principal religions to which these concepts particularly apply. In addition, the publication provides the following units of work for enquiring into concepts that are of particular significance to some of the major world religions: **sacrifice** for Christianity, **suffering** for Buddhism, **devotion** for Hinduism, **revelation** for Islam, **freedom** for Judaism and **service** for Sikhism. The accompanying CD provides support material, pictures, drawing and writing frames for teaching the units of work. These materials can be used on the whiteboard or duplicated and used as hard copies for pupils. Teachers might:

- follow the guidance in the book for a particular concept in relation to Christianity, going through all the elements in the cycle (**communicate**, **apply**, **enquire**, **contextualise** and **evaluate**) and then illustrate the same concept within the **contextualise** and **evaluate** elements of another religion on which they wish to focus.
- follow the guidance for the **communicate**, **apply** and **enquire** elements in the book for a particular concept and then follow the guidance for the same concept in the **contextualise** and **evaluate** elements for the religion on which they wish to focus, leaving out the Christian dimension on this occasion
- select from the units of work for any of the six concepts which relate particularly to each of the major faiths provided (see pages 99–127).

It is not appropriate to exemplify every concept within all religions, because the concept may not have the same significance in every religion. Illustrative material has been included where there are appropriate and accessible examples from the religions identified.

Teachers will need to consult their locally agreed syllabus for RE in order to find out which religion they should be exploring at KS 2. If the agreed syllabus requires that a school can choose a religion to explore, it is recommended that pupils should consistently meet aspects and examples of that religion within a year group at KS 2 so as to help pupils to develop a coherent picture of that religion alongside their learning about Christianity. Experience tells us that dropping into a number of different religions can cause confusion.

The units have been planned so that pupils progress in their understanding as they move around the cycle of learning, so the correct order and inclusion of all the five elements in the cycle is essential for effective learning.

Concepts for exploration

Community in Christianity
Community in Buddhism, Hinduism, Islam, Judaism and Sikhism
God in Christianity
God in Hinduism, Islam, Judaism and Sikhism
Holy in Christianity, through looking at Mary, Mother of God
Holy through the Holy Torah scrolls in Judaism
Symbol in Christianity
Symbol through the image of the Buddha in Buddhism, through the symbol of water of the River Ganges in Hinduism, through the wearing of Ihram in Islam, through the bread at Shabbat in Judaism, and through the Kirpan in Sikhism
Ritual in Christianity through the Eucharist
Ritual through puja in Buddhism, through arti in Hinduism, through salah in Islam, through the use of tefillin in Judaism, and through the amrit ceremony to join the Khalsa in Sikhism
Sacrifice through the Easter story in Christianity
Suffering through the teachings of the Buddha in Buddhism
Devotion through looking at the worship of devotees to Krishna in Hinduism
Revelation through looking at Muhammad's revelation in Islam
Freedom through the celebration of Passover in Judaism
Service through looking at some of the beliefs and practices in Sikhism

Concept: *community*

In this unit pupils enquire into the concept of *community*. All pupils will have their own experiences of *community*, the school being the most obvious one. Many will also have experiences of communities outside school such as Brownies or Cubs, sports clubs or youth clubs. Some pupils may also be part of religious communities. This unit enables pupils to recognise features of communities, their value to those who belong, and any issues that are raised for insiders and those outside communities. The core religious reference material is drawn from Christianity, followed by examples of how *community* can be explored within aspects of other major religions.

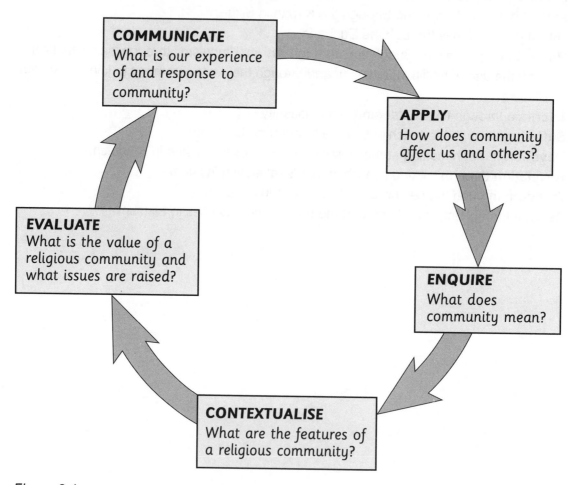

COMMUNICATE
What is our experience of and response to community?

APPLY
How does community affect us and others?

EVALUATE
What is the value of a religious community and what issues are raised?

ENQUIRE
What does community mean?

CONTEXTUALISE
What are the features of a religious community?

Figure 2.1

What is the value of *community* for Buddhists?
What is the value of *community* for Hindus?
What is the value of *community* for Muslims?
What is the value of *community* for Jews?
What is the value of *community* for Sikhs?

What is the value of the Christian *Community* for Christians?

Step 1 Enquire

What does *community* mean?

- Pupils in small groups brainstorm the word *community*. What does it mean? What are the characteristics of a *community*?
- Pupils compare their ideas with other groups. Are there any similarities? Are there any surprises?
- The teacher should collate pupils' ideas and draw out the features and characteristics of a *community* (such as a shared interest, a uniform or symbol, a meeting place, a set of rules, some rituals, a hierarchy or system of authority).
- Pupils complete a simple writing frame, 'A *community* is …' (see Figure 2.2 also available on the CD).

A community is............

Figure 2.2

- The teacher should show a picture of Christians together (see the CD artwork 1), and ask pupils to speculate about which *community* the people in the picture belong to. What clues are there in the picture?

Step 2 Contextualise

What are the features of a Christian *community*?

Pupils in pairs or small groups could research different features of a Christian *community* (church) to present to the whole class, or the teacher may wish to lead all the pupils systematically through the enquiry.

- Remind pupils of the features/characteristics of a community identified in Step 1, such as **shared interest, a uniform or symbol, a meeting place, a set of rules, some rituals, a hierarchy or system of authority.**
- Visit a local church (the *community* meeting place), and the teacher direct pupils to look for clues about what happens in a Christian *community* and any expressions of beliefs identified.

- A few members of the church should be available during the visit to answer pupils' questions about what happens in that Christian *community* and the purpose of those activities.
- Pupils can take digital pictures or sketch points of interest and make notes about them. (See CD artwork 2 and 4 for examples).

Questions to pursue

- Do members of the *community* wear any signs or symbols that remind them that they belong to that *community*?
- What activities go on here that help people to feel part of the *community*?
- How are the chairs arranged? Does this help the feeling of *community*?
- What is the focal point in the church? What does that say about what the *community* is meeting together to think about?
- Is there any sign of music in the church? What does that tell you about the activities of the *community*?
- What is the atmosphere like in the church? How does that help the *community*?
- Look at the prayer books and the hymn books on the seats or the pews, or perhaps piled up at the back of the church. What does this tell you about the activities of the *community*?
- What is the purpose of the ritual of sharing bread and wine every Sunday? How does that help the *community*?
- Where is the Bible kept? What does this say about how important it is for the *community*?
- Look at the notice board inside the church or in the church porch or entrance. What activities are arranged for the *community*? (These might include Bible reading groups, youth clubs, Sunday school, money raising activities, baptisms, marriages and funerals.) What does that tell you about what is important for that *community*?
- Is there a church hall? How is that used by the Christian *community*? (Perhaps for meetings, coffee after the Sunday service, youth club.) How do those activities help the *community*?
- Is there any evidence of rules within the *community*? Where do they come from? Are the rules enforced? Are people who break the rules allowed to stay within the *community*?

- In the classroom pupils should create a display about the local Christian *community* with their pictures and labels of explanation.
- Invite a priest or minister to answer pupils' questions about the vestments worn and their purpose within their *community*.
- Invite the visiting priest or minister to talk about the hierarchy within their *community* and how that helps or hinders the functioning of the *community*.

Step 3 Evaluate

What is the value of the Christian *community* to members and what issues are raised?

- Pupils in pairs should role play a Christian trying to convince a friend that they should belong to the Christian *community*. One pupil should focus on the value and advantages of belonging to that *community,* while their partner asks questions. They then swap roles.
- The teacher should draw together key points that arose from the role play and any issues that were raised.
- Print out and prepare sets of the cards shown as Figure 2.3 (also see the CD). Pupils 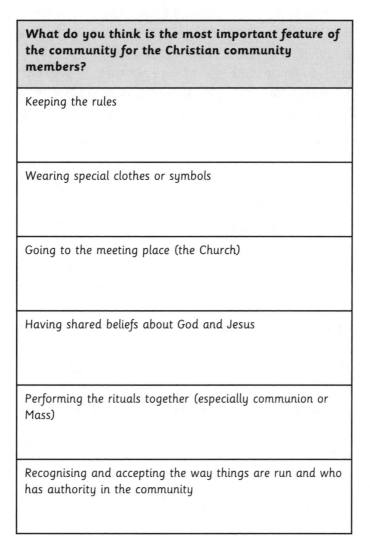 in pairs sort them into an order of priority.

What do you think is the most important feature of the community for the Christian community members?
Keeping the rules
Wearing special clothes or symbols
Going to the meeting place (the Church)
Having shared beliefs about God and Jesus
Performing the rituals together (especially communion or Mass)
Recognising and accepting the way things are run and who has authority in the community

Figure 2.3

- Pupils should compare their order of priority with other pairs. Are there any similarities or differences? Pupils explain the reasons for their decisions.
- Instruct the pupils to remove the feature that they, in their pairs, consider to be the least important. Could a Christian refuse to participate in that feature and still be part of the Christian *community*? How might other Christians in the *community* react?
- The teacher should encourage class discussion about some of the issues that are raised.

Questions to prompt discussion

- Can anyone become a member of a Christian *community*? Why or why not?
- What might stop someone joining a Christian *community*?
- What might persuade someone to join a Christian *community*?
- What do you think are the advantages of belonging to a Christian *community*?
- What are the disadvantages?
- Do you think that there are times or circumstances when someone wants to be part of the Christian *community* more than at others? Why might that be?
- Do you think it would be easy to join a Christian *community*? Why? Why not?
- Which is the most important feature of the *community* that members should adopt (such as the shared beliefs, going to the meeting place, wearing the symbols, performing the rituals, keeping the rules)?
- Could someone continue to be part of the *community* if they did not adopt one of the features (for instance, they broke the rules, did not wear the symbols, did not share the beliefs or did not take part in the rituals)?

Step 4 Communicate

What is our experience of and response to *community*?

- Pupils discuss in pairs the features of a community to which they belong, such as the school, a youth club, a football team, karate club, Brownies or Cubs (identifying the shared beliefs/interests, the uniform/badge, the rituals, the rules and so on).
- Pupils bring in pictures of themselves or draw themselves in their communities and list the identified features.
- Pupils talk about their feelings in that *community* in groups and then class discussion, or:
- Through class discussion pupils should create their class as a *community* and decide on:
  - a shared interest or belief (for instance, reduce their carbon footprint or stop bullying)
  - a badge or logo
  - a ritual
  - a meeting place
  - a hierarchy or system of organisation
  - rules
  - activities.
- Create a class display to show features of the *community* created and developed.

Step 5 Apply

How does *community* affect us and others?

- The teacher should duplicate and distribute the cards (see Figure 2.4. and CD) to each pupil. Pupils place them in order of priority for themselves.

What is the most important feature of your community for you?
Keeping the rules
Wearing the uniform or symbol
Going to the meeting place
Having shared beliefs or interests with other people
Performing the rituals together
Recognising and accepting the way things are run and who has authority

Figure 2.4

- Pupils should share their responses in groups and discuss the reasons for their priorities.
- Share the discussions as a class.

Questions to prompt discussion

- What do you like most about the *community* that you belong to?
- What makes people want to be part of a *community*?
- Are there any features of the *community* that you do not like? What? Why?
- Could you change anything about your *community*? How?
- What would happen to a person who did not want to participate in a feature of the *community* (for instance, came to school dressed like a Goth, went to Karate and refused to do the Karate bow, went to Cubs and argued with the leader all the time)?
- How would you feel if you were not allowed to be part of a *community* that you wanted to join?
- Are there some communities that you would not ever want to join? What? Why?

(▶)   • Pupils complete the writing frame shown in Figure 2.5 (also see the CD).

```
┌─────────────────────────────────────────────┐
│                                               │
│    Good things about a community are........  │
│                                               │
│                                               │
│                                               │
│                                               │
│                                               │
│                                               │
│                                               │
│                                               │
│    Some negative things about a community are.........│
│                                               │
│                                               │
│                                               │
│                                               │
│                                               │
│                                               │
│                                               │
│                                               │
│                                               │
└─────────────────────────────────────────────┘
```

Figure 2.5

Community in Buddhism

What is the value of *community* for Buddhists?

Pupils should explore Step 1 in the book (page 9) before they engage with Steps 2 and 3 in this section. This should then be followed by Steps 4 and 5 in the book (pages 12–13).

Step 2 Contextualise

What are the important features of a Buddhist *community*?

• Pupils in pairs or small groups could research different features of a Buddhist *community* (sangha) to present to the whole class, or the teacher might wish to lead all the pupils systematically through the enquiry.

• Remind pupils of the features/characteristics of a *community* identified in Step 1, such as **shared interests, a uniform or symbol, a meeting place, a set of rules, some rituals, a hierarchy or system of authority.**

• Visit a sangha if possible (the Buddhist *community* of monks and nuns) or a virtual sangha, and the teacher should direct pupils to look for clues about what happens in (▶)   a Buddhist *community* and expressions of beliefs (see CD artwork 6 and 7).

- Pupils can make notes about points of interest.

Questions to pursue

- Do members of the *community* wear any signs or symbols that remind them that they belong to that *community*?
- What activities go on here that help people to feel part of the *community*?
- How is the meeting room arranged? Does this help the feeling of *community*?
- What is the focal point in the meeting room? What does that say about what the *community* is meeting together to think about?
- Is there any sign of the sort of activities that go on in the room? What is the atmosphere like in the room? How does that help the *community*?
- What is the purpose of the ritual of presenting offerings in front of the statue of the Buddha? How does that help the *community*?
- Is there a notice board inside the building? What activities are arranged for the *community* (such as meditation sessions, retreats, talks, children's days or festival celebrations)? What does that tell you about what is important for that *community*?
- Is there any evidence of rules within the *community*? Where do they come from? Are the rules enforced? Are people who break the rules allowed to stay within the *community*?

- In the classroom pupils create a display about a Buddhist *community* with pictures and labels of explanation.
- Invite a Buddhist monk or nun to answer pupils' questions about their role within their *community*.
- Invite the Buddhist to talk about the hierarchy in their *community* and how that helps or hinders the functioning of the *community*.

Step 3 Evaluate

What is the value of the Buddhist *community* to members and what issues are raised?

- Pupils in pairs role play a Buddhist trying to convince their friend that they should belong to a Buddhist *community*. One pupil should focus on the value and advantages of belonging to that *community,* while the partner asks questions. The pupils then swap roles.
- Draw together key points that arise from the role play and any issues that are raised.
- Print out and prepare sets of the cards shown as Figure 2.6 and on the CD, and pupils ◀ in pairs sort them into an order of priority.
- Pupils compare their order of priority with other pairs. Are there any similarities or differences? Pupils should explain the reasons for their decisions.
- Instruct the pupils to remove the feature that they consider to be the least important. Could a Buddhist refuse to participate in that feature and still be part of the Buddhist *community*? How might other Buddhists in the *community* react?
- The teacher should encourage class discussion about some of the issues that are raised.

What do you think is the most important feature of the community for the Buddhist community members?
Keeping the rules
The monks wearing the special clothes
Going to the meeting place (the temple or Vihara)
Having shared beliefs about the Buddha and his teachings
Performing the rituals together
Recognising and accepting the way things are run and who has authority in the community

Figure 2.6

Questions to prompt discussion

- Can anyone become a member of a Buddhist *community*? Why? Why not?
- What might stop someone joining a Buddhist *community*?
- What might persuade someone to join a Buddhist *community*?
- What do you think are the advantages of belonging to a Buddhist *community*?
- What are the disadvantages?
- Do you think that there are times or circumstances when someone wants to be part of the Buddhist *community* more than at others? Why might that be?
- Do you think it would be easy to join a Buddhist *community*? Why? Why not?
- Which is the most important feature of the *community* that members should adopt (such as the shared beliefs, going to the meeting place, wearing the symbols, performing the rituals, keeping the rules)?
- Could someone continue to be part of the *community* if they did not adopt one of the features (for example if they broke the rules, did not wear the symbols, did not share the beliefs or did not take part in the rituals)?

Go to Steps 4 and 5 in the book (pages 12–13) to complete the cycle.

Community in Hinduism

What is the value of *community* for Hindus?

Pupils should explore Step 1 in the book (page 9) before they engage with Steps 2 and 3 in this section. This should then be followed by Steps 4 and 5 in the book (pages 12–13).

Step 2 Contextualise

What are the important features of a Hindu *community*?

Pupils in pairs or small groups could research different features of a Hindu *community* to present to the whole class, or teachers may wish to lead all the pupils, systematically, through the enquiry.

- Remind pupils of the features/characteristics of a *community* identified in Step 1, such as a **shared interest, a uniform or symbol, a meeting place, a set of rules, some rituals, a hierarchy or system of authority.**
- Visit a Hindu temple (a mandir) if possible, or a virtual mandir. and the teacher should direct pupils to look for clues about what happens in a Hindu *community* and expressions of beliefs (see CD artwork 8 and 9).
- Pupils can make notes about points of interest.

Questions to pursue

- Do members of the *community* wear any signs, symbols or special clothes that remind them that they belong to that *community*?
- What activities go on here that help people to feel part of the *community*?
- How is the meeting room arranged? Does this help the feeling of *community*?
- What is the focal point in the meeting room? What does that say about what the *community* is meeting together to think about?
- What is the atmosphere like in the room? How does that help the *community*?
- Are there any signs that music is played in the *community*? What does that tell you about some of their activities?
- What is the purpose of the ritual of presenting offerings? How does that show what is important to the *community*?
- Is there a notice board inside the building? What activities are arranged for the *community* (such as talks, children's days or festival celebrations)? What does that tell you about what is important for that *community*?
- Is there any evidence of rules within the *community*? Where do they come from? Are the rules enforced? Are people who break the rules allowed to stay within the *community*?

- In the classroom pupils create a display about a Hindu *community* with pictures and labels of explanation.
- Invite a Hindu visitor to answer pupils' questions about their role within their *community*.

● Invite the Hindu visitor to talk about the hierarchy in their *community* and how that helps or hinders the functioning of the *community*.

Step 3 Evaluate

What is the value of the Hindu *community* to members and what issues are raised?

● Pupils in pairs role play a Hindu trying to convince their friend that they should belong to a Hindu *community*. One pupil should focus on the value and advantages of belonging to that *community,* while the partner asks questions. The pupils then swap roles.
● Draw together key points that arise from the role play and any issues that are raised.
● Print out and prepare sets of the cards shown as Figure 2.7 and on the CD. Pupils in pairs sort them into an order of priority.
● Pupils compare their order of priority with other pairs. Are there any similarities or differences? Pupils should explain the reasons for their decisions.
● Instruct the pupils to remove the feature that they consider to be the least important. Could a Hindu refuse to participate in that feature and still be part of the Hindu *community*? How might other Hindus in the *community* react?
● The teacher should encourage class discussion about some of the issues that are raised.

What do you think is the most important feature of the community for the Hindu community members?
Keeping the rules
Wearing special clothes or symbols
Going to the meeting place (the Mandir)
Having shared beliefs about God and karma
Performing the rituals together (e.g. sharing Prashad)
Recognising and accepting the way things are run and who has authority in the community

Figure 2.7

Questions to prompt discussion

- Can anyone become a member of a Hindu *community*? Why? Why not?
- What might stop someone joining a Hindu *community*?
- What might persuade someone to join a Hindu *community*?
- What do you think are the advantages of belonging to a Hindu *community*?
- What are the disadvantages?
- Do you think that there are times or circumstances when someone wants to be part of the Hindu *community* more than at others? Why might that be?
- Do you think it would be easy to join a Hindu *community*? Why? Why not?
- Which is the most important feature of the *community* that members should adopt (such as shared beliefs, going to the meeting place, wearing the symbols, performing the rituals or keeping the rules)?
- Could someone continue to be part of the *community* if they did not adopt one of the features (for instance if they broke the rules, did not wear the symbols, did not share the beliefs or did not take part in the rituals)?

Go to Steps 4 and 5 in the book (pages 12–13) to complete the cycle.

Community in Judaism

What is the value of *community* for Jews?

Pupils should explore Step 1 in the book (page 9) before they engage with Steps 2 and 3 in this section. This should then be followed by Steps 4 and 5 in the book (pages 12–13).

Step 2 Contextualise

What are the important features of a Jewish *community*?

Pupils in pairs or small groups could research different features of a Jewish *community* to present to the whole class, or the teachers might wish to lead all the pupils, systematically, through the enquiry.

- Remind pupils of the features/characteristics of a *community* identified in Step 1, such as **a shared interest, a uniform or symbol, a meeting place, a set of rules, some rituals, a hierarchy or system of authority.**
- Visit a synagogue if possible, or a virtual synagogue, and the teacher direct pupils to look for clues about what happens in a Jewish *community* (see CD artwork 11, 12, ◀ 13).
- Pupils can make notes about points of interest.

Questions to pursue

- Do members of the *community* wear any signs, symbols or special clothes that remind them that they belong to that *community*?
- What activities go on here that help people to feel part of the *community*?
- How is the meeting room arranged? Does this help the feeling of *community*?
- What is the focal point in the meeting room? What does that say about what the *community* is meeting together to think about?
- Is there any sign of the sort of activities that go on in the room? What is the atmosphere like in the room? How does that help the *community*?
- What is the purpose of the ritual of taking the Torah scroll out of the Ark, undressing it and placing it on the bimah? How does that show what is important to the *community*?
- Is there a notice board inside the building? What activities are arranged for the *community* (such as *community* meetings, talks, children's days or festival celebrations)? What does that tell you about what is important for that *community*?
- Is there any evidence of rules within the *community*? Where do they come from? Are the rules enforced? Are people who break the rules allowed to stay within the *community*?

- In the classroom pupils create a display about a Jewish *community* with pictures and labels of explanation.
- Invite a Jewish visitor to answer pupils' questions about their role within their *community*.
- Invite the Jewish visitor to talk about the hierarchy in their *community* and how that helps or hinders the functioning of the *community*.

Step 3 Evaluate

What is the value of the Jewish *community* to members and what issues are raised?

- Pupils in pairs role play a Jew trying to convince their friend that they should attend meetings with the Jewish community. One pupil should focus on the value and advantages of belonging to that *community,* while the partner asks questions. The pupils then swap roles.
- Draw together key points that arise from the role play and any issues that are raised.
- Print out and prepare sets of the cards shown as Figure 2.8 and on the CD . Pupils in pairs sort them into an order of priority.
- Pupils should compare their order of priority with other pairs. Are there any similarities or differences? Pupils should explain the reasons for their decisions.
- Instruct the pupils to remove the feature that they consider to be the least important. Could a Jew refuse to participate in that feature and still be part of the Jewish *community*? How might other Jews in the *community* react?
- The teacher should encourage class discussion about some of the issues that are raised.

Note that Jews are considered to be a race of people, and Jews are born into their faith by having a Jewish mother. However, many synagogues accept converts to Judaism. A Jewish person will not necessarily be an active member of a Jewish *community*.

Questions to prompt discussion

- Can anyone become a member of a Jewish *community*? Why? Why not?
- What might stop someone joining a Jewish *community*?
- What might persuade someone to join a Jewish *community*?
- What do you think are the advantages of belonging to a Jewish *community*?
- What are the disadvantages?
- Do you think that there are times or circumstances when someone wants to be part of the Jewish *community* more than at others? Why might that be?
- Do you think it would be easy to join a Jewish *community*? Why? Why not?
- Which is the most important feature of the *community* that members should adopt (such as the shared beliefs, going to the meeting place, wearing the symbols, performing the rituals, keeping the rules)?
- Could someone continue to be part of the *community* if they did not adopt one of the features (for instance if they broke the rules, did not wear the symbols, did not share the beliefs or did not take part in the rituals)?

What do you think is the most important feature of the community for the Jewish community members?
Keeping the rules
Wearing special clothes or symbols
Going to the meeting place (the synagogue)
Having shared beliefs about God
Performing the rituals together (e.g. touching the Mezuzah as they enter)
Recognising and accepting the way things are run and who has authority in the community

Figure 2.8

Go to Steps 4 and 5 in the book (pages 12–13) to complete the cycle.

Community in Islam

What is the value of *community* for Muslims?

Pupils should explore Step 1 in the book (page 9) before they engage with Steps 2 and 3 in this section. This should then be followed by Steps 4 and 5 in the book (pages 12–13)

Step 2 Contextualise

What are the important features of a Muslim *community*?

- Pupils in pairs or small groups could research different features of a Muslim *community* to present to the whole class, or the teacher might wish to lead all the pupils, systematically, through the enquiry.
- Remind pupils of the features/characteristics of a *community* identified in Step 1, such as **a shared interest, a uniform or symbol, a meeting place, a set of rules, some rituals, a hierarchy or system of authority.**
- Visit a mosque if possible, or a virtual mosque, and the teacher direct pupils to look for clues about what happens in a Muslim *community* (see CD artwork 14, 15, 16 and 17).
- Pupils can make notes about points of interest.

Questions to pursue

- Do members of the *community* wear any signs, symbols or special clothes that remind them that they belong to that *community*?
- What activities go on here that help people to feel part of the *community*?
- How is the meeting room arranged? Does this help the feeling of *community*?
- What is the focal point in the meeting room? What does that say about what the *community* is meeting together to think about?
- Is there any sign of the sort of activities that go on in the room? What is the atmosphere like in the room? How does that help the *community*?
- What is the purpose of the prayer ritual (*salah*)? How does that show what is important to the *community*?
- Is there a notice board inside the building? What activities are arranged for the *community* (such as *community* meetings, talks, children's days or festival celebrations)? What does that tell you about what is important for that *community*?
- Is there any evidence of rules within the *community*? Where do they come from? Are the rules enforced? Are people who break the rules allowed to stay within the *community*?

- In the classroom pupils create a display about a Muslim *community* with pictures and labels of explanation.
- Invite a Muslim visitor to answer pupils' questions about their role within their *community*.
- Invite the Muslim visitor to talk about the hierarchy in their *community* and how that helps or hinders the functioning of the *community*.

Step 3 Evaluate

What is the value of the Muslim *community* to members and what issues are raised?

- Pupils in pairs role play a Muslim trying to convince their friend that they should belong to a Muslim *community*. One pupil should focus on the value and advantages of belonging to that *community,* while the partner asks questions. The pupils then swap roles.
- Draw together key points that arise from the role play and any issues that are raised.
- Print out and prepares sets of the cards shown as Figure 2.9 and on the CD. Pupils in ◀ pairs sort them into an order of priority.
- Pupils compare their order of priority with other pairs. Are there any similarities or differences? Pupils should explain the reasons for their decisions.
- Instruct the pupils to remove the feature that they consider to be the least important. Could a Muslim refuse to participate in that feature and still be part of the Muslim *community*? How might other Muslims in the *community* react?
- The teacher should encourage class discussion about some of the issues that are raised.

What do you think is the most important feature of the community for the Muslim community members?
Keeping the rules
Wearing special clothes or symbols
Going to the meeting place (the Mosque)
Having shared beliefs about Allah
Performing the rituals together (e.g. praying)
Recognising and accepting the way things are run and who has authority in the community

Figure 2.9

Questions to prompt discussion

- Can anyone become a member of a Muslim *community*? Why? Why not?
- What might stop someone joining a Muslim *community*?
- What might persuade someone to join a Muslim *community*?
- What do you think are the advantages of belonging to a Muslim *community*?
- What are the disadvantages?
- Do you think that there are times or circumstances when someone wants to be part of the Muslim *community* more than at others? Why might that be?
- Do you think it would be easy to join a Muslim *community*? Why/Why not?
- Which is the most important feature of the *community* that members should adopt (such as the shared beliefs, going to the meeting place, wearing the symbols, performing the rituals and keeping the rules)?
- Could someone continue to be part of the *community* if they did not adopt one of the features (for instance if they broke the rules, did not wear the symbols, did not share the beliefs or did not take part in the rituals)?

Go to Steps 4 and 5 in the book (pages 12–13) to complete the cycle.

Community in Sikhism

What is the value of *community* for Sikhs?

Pupils should explore Step 1 in the book (page 9) before they engage with Steps 2 and 3 in this section. This should then be followed by Steps 4 and 5 in the book (pages 12–13).

Step 2 Contextualise

What are the important features of a Sikh *community*?

Pupils in pairs or small groups could research different features of a Sikh *community* to present to the whole class, or the teacher might wish to lead all the pupils, systematically, through the enquiry.

- Remind pupils of the features/characteristics of a *community* identified in Step 1, such as **a shared interest, a uniform or symbol, a meeting place, a set of rules, some rituals, a hierarchy or system of authority.**
- Visit a gurdwara if possible, or a virtual gurdwara, and the teacher direct pupils to look for clues about what happens in a Sikh *community* (see CD artwork 18, 19 and 20).
- Pupils can make notes about points of interest.
- In the classroom pupils create a display about a Sikh *community* with pictures and labels of explanation.
- Invite a Sikh visitor to answer pupils' questions about their role within their *community*.

- Invite the Sikh visitor to talk about the hierarchy in their *community* and how that helps or hinders the functioning of the *community*.

Questions to pursue

- Do members of the *community* wear any signs, symbols or special clothes that remind them that they belong to that *community*?
- What activities go on here that help people to feel part of the *community*?
- How is the meeting room arranged? Does this help the feeling of *community*?
- What is the focal point in the meeting room? What does that say about what the *community* is meeting together to think about?
- Is there any sign of the sort of activities that go on in the room? What is the atmosphere like in the room? How does that help the *community*?
- What is the purpose of waving the chauri over the Guru Granth Sahib? How does that show what is important to the *community*?
- What do you think is the purpose of the *community* kitchen and eating area? What does that tell you about the *community*?
- Is there a notice board inside the building? What activities are arranged for the *community* (such as *community* meetings, talks, charity work, children's days or festival celebrations)? What does that tell you about what is important for that *community*?
- Is there any evidence of rules within the *community*? Where do they come from? Are the rules enforced? Are people who break the rules allowed to stay within the *community*?

Step 3 Evaluate

What is the value of the Sikh *community* to members and what issues are raised?

- Pupils in pairs role play a Sikh trying to convince their friend that they should belong to a Sikh *community*. One pupil should focus on the value and advantages of belonging to that *community* while the partner asks questions. The pupils then swap roles.
- Draw together key points that arise from the role play and any issues that are raised.
- Print out and prepare sets of the cards shown as Figure 2.10 and on the CD. Pupils in pairs to sort them into an order of priority.
- Pupils should compare their order of priority with other pairs. Are there any similarities or differences? Pupils should explain the reasons for their decisions.
- Instruct the pupils to remove the feature that they consider to be the least important. Could a Sikh refuse to participate in that feature and still be part of the Sikh *community*? How might other Sikhs in the *community* react?
- The teacher should encourage class discussion about some of the issues that are raised.

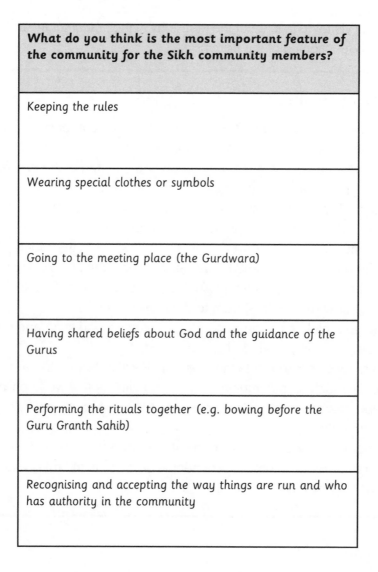

What do you think is the most important feature of the community for the Sikh community members?
Keeping the rules
Wearing special clothes or symbols
Going to the meeting place (the Gurdwara)
Having shared beliefs about God and the guidance of the Gurus
Performing the rituals together (e.g. bowing before the Guru Granth Sahib)
Recognising and accepting the way things are run and who has authority in the community

Figure 2.10

Questions to prompt discussion

- Can anyone become a member of a Sikh *community*? Why? Why not?
- What might stop someone joining a Sikh *community*?
- What might persuade someone to join a Sikh *community*?
- What do you think are the advantages of belonging to a Sikh *community*?
- What are the disadvantages?
- Do you think that there are times or circumstances when someone wants to be part of the Sikh *community* more than at others? Why might that be?
- Do you think it would be easy to join a Sikh *community*? Why? Why not?
- Which is the most important feature of the *community* that members should adopt (such as the shared beliefs, going to the meeting place, wearing the symbols, performing the rituals or keeping the rules)?
- Could someone continue to be part of the *community* if they did not adopt one of the features (for instance if they broke the rules, did not wear the symbols, did not share the beliefs or did not take part in the rituals)?

Go to Steps 4 and 5 in the book (pages 12–13) to complete the cycle.

Resources on the CD

Figures

2.2   Writing frame – *A community is*
2.3   Cards – important features of *community* for Christians
2.4   Cards – important features of *community* for you
2.5   Writing frame – Good/negative things about a community
2.6   Cards – important features of *community* for Buddhists
2.7   Cards – important features of *community* for Hindus
2.8   Cards – important features of *community* for Jews
2.9   Cards – important features of *community* for Muslims
2.10 Cards – important features of *community* for Sikhs

Artwork

1.   Christians together
2.   Church
4.   Organist
6.   Praying in front of Buddha
7.   A sangha
8.   A mandir
9.   Taking off shoes at the mandir
11. A synagogue
12. Praying in the synagogue
13. A mezuzah.
14. Muslim men worshipping
15. Learning to read Arabic in the mosque
16. Women praying in the mosque
17. Giving Zakat in the mosque
18. Worshipping in the gurdwara
19. Taking off shoes in the gurwara
20. Sharing food in the langar

Concept: God

This unit of work enables pupils to enquire into a group B concept, which is a concept that is common to many religions and used in the study of religion (see Figure 1.1, page 3). At no time during this enquiry should pupils feel there is any expectation that they should believe or not believe in a God. The unit encourages an open, philosophical investigation into different ideas that people have about God, and enables pupils to reflect on and express their own responses from an informed position. The book provides opportunities to investigate Christian views of God and views of God within some of the major world faiths.

The Christian view of God
The Hindu view of God
The Muslim view of God
The Jewish view of God
The Sikh view of God

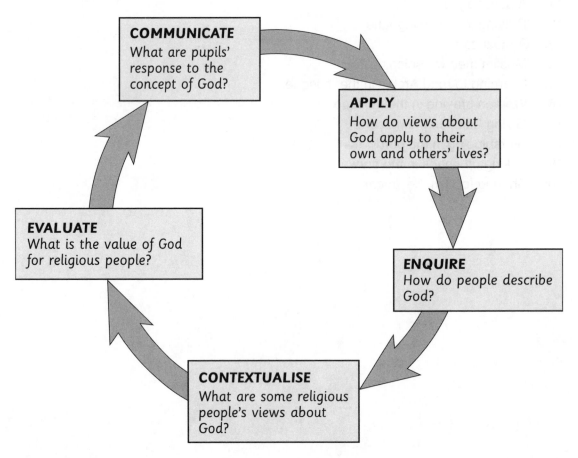

Figure 3.1

The Christian view of God

Step 1 Enquire

How do people describe God?

● Pupils in groups should brainstorm on A3 sheets ways in which people describe God. (Note: the teacher should not ask for pupils' personal beliefs about God at this stage.) Ideas should be recorded on a whiteboard or the A3 sheets pinned up so they can be compared.

> **Questions to prompt discussion**
>
> ● Was this an easy task? Why? Why not?
> ● Can you see any groupings of the descriptions? Can they be classified in any way?
> ● Are there any descriptions that contradict others? Does that matter? Are you surprised by that?
> ● Are there any descriptions that you have not heard before?
> ● Are there some descriptions that you find particularly interesting or surprising?
> ● What have you discovered by doing the activity?
> ● What have you learned about the ways in which people describe God?

● Pupils should choose one of the descriptions of God and produce some artwork or a poem expressing the description they have selected. The results should be displayed and discussed by the class.

> **Questions to prompt discussion**
>
> ● What description of God do you think this picture/poem is about?
> ● What is it about the picture/poem that tells us that?
> ● Does anyone have any suggestions about how it might be improved?

Step 2 Contextualise

What are the Christian views about God?

● Duplicate and distribute some hymns and prayers which make reference to the nature of God (see the CD and Figure 3.2) or names/descriptions of God. Pupils should high- light the names and descriptions. Discuss and explain difficult words, and pupils make notes.

Eternal Father, Spirit,
Word, Praise to the Lord
of my salvation, Salvation
is of Christ the Lord.

Patrick of Ireland

May Jesus Christ, the king
of glory, help us to make
the right use of all the
myrrh that God sends, and
to offer to him the true
incense of our hearts.

Johann Tauler

O most high, Almighty,
good Lord God, to you
belong praise, glory,
honour, and all blessing!

Francis of Assisi

You, O eternal Trinity, are
a deep sea, into which the
more I enter the more I
find, and the more I find
the more I seek.

Catherine of Siena

You are holy, Lord, the
only God and your deeds
are wonderful. You are
strong, you are great.
You are the most High,
you are almighty.

Francis of Assisi

Almighty and everlasting
God, you hate nothing that
you have made, and forgive
the sins of all those who
are penitent.

Thomas Cranmer

Figure 3.2a

Oh most merciful
Redeemer, Friend and
Brother, may we know thee
more clearly, love thee more
dearly, and follow thee
more nearly, day by day.

Richard,
Bishop of Chichester

O Lord, heavenly Father,
in whom is the fullness of
light and wisdom, en-
lighten our minds by your
Holy Spirit.

John Calvin

Worthy is the Lamb, who
was slain, to receive power
and wealth and wisdom
and strength and honour
and glory and praise!

Revelations

Oh God the Father of the
forsaken, the help of the
weak, the supplier of the
needy;...

Lord Shaftesbury

Flame-dancing Spirit,
come Sweep us off our feet
and dance us through our
days

St. Hilda Community
(Women Included, SPCK 1991)

Oh God the Father of all
you ask every one of us to
spread love

Mother Theresa and
Brother Roger

Figure 3.2b

Questions to prompt discussion

- Which do you think is the most commonly used description or name of God used by Christians? Why do you think that is?
- Are there any names/descriptions which surprise you? Why?
- Are there some names/descriptions that you don't understand?
- Can anyone guess what that might mean?
- Do you think that is a good description/name for God? Why? Why not?
- Have you found any metaphors or similes for God?

- Pupils produce a glossary of terms which could be used at the back of a hymnbook or prayer book (literacy link) explaining the names and descriptions used for God in Christianity.
- Pupils in pairs or small groups investigate Bible stories from the selection (see the CD and pages 32–35). The teacher might wish to duplicate and distribute the texts.

Questions to prompt discussion

- What can we know about the Christian view of God from this story?
- Does anything in this story surprise you?
- Is God different in different stories? How?

- Each pair/group share their findings with the rest of the class.
- Pupils should write a simple play script to retell the story, or
  write a character profile of God as shown in the story, or
  produce an annotated drawing illustrating what God is like in the story.
- Explore the Christian belief in the Holy Trinity, and discuss which of the stories is associated with each dimension of the Trinity (Father, Son and Holy Spirit).

Questions to prompt discussion

- Which story or stories do you think describe God as the Father?
- Which story or stories do you think describe God as the Son (Jesus)?
- Which story or stories do you think describe God as the Holy Spirit?
- Does anyone disagree with that choice? Can you think of a better story that expresses the ideas of Father/Son/Holy Spirit?

- Pupils produce a diagram or a simple image for a poster which could be put outside a church to explain the Holy Trinity.
- Alternatively, pupils should complete the writing frame. See Figure 3.3. (See CD).

{GOD}   Name: ....

Here are some of the ways Christians describe God...

Christians believe God to be "3 in 1" – the Holy Trinity.
Write down what the three parts are and explain what they
mean.

Parts of the Trinity	Meaning
1.	
2.	
3.	

This is a Bible story which shows God as part of the
Trinity...

This story shows God as: ....

Figure 3.3

God calls to Moses from a burning bush

Moses worked for his father in law, and was taking care of his sheep and goats in
the desert when he came to a mountain called Sinai. Flames suddenly started flick-
ering in a bush nearby. Wondering what was causing the fire, Moses went closer to
look and saw, to his amazement, that the bush was not burning up, and that the
flames did not harm the bush.

As Moses moved closer still he heard a thunderous voice call to him.

'Moses! Moses!' called the voice.

Moses answered, 'Yes, here I am.'

'Don't come any closer.' called the voice. 'You must take your shoes off because
you are on Holy ground. I am God,' called the voice.

Moses was terrified and cowered on the ground covering his face. He was frightened of seeing God.

Then God spoke again. 'I know that my people in Egypt are being treated cruelly.
I have heard them calling out to be saved from the Egyptians who use them as
slaves. I have come to rescue them from the Egyptians. I will take them to a land
which is rich and fertile.'

God protects Daniel in the pit of lions

Daniel had an important role working for a king. He was a supervisor of King Darius' governors. King Darius had noticed that Daniel was a good, honest, hardworking man who was always reliable, so he liked him and trusted him. This, however, made the other supervisors and governors jealous. They did not like Daniel being the favourite, and they set about planning his downfall.

These men knew that there was nothing more important to Daniel than his religion and praying to his God. Very cleverly, they persuaded the king to make a new law. The law stated that within the following 30 days anyone requesting anything from man or God, and not from Darius the king, would be thrown in a pit of lions. King Darius agreed to the new law and signed the decree.

Now, because Daniel was a religious man and praying to God was more important than anything else to him, he continued to pray every day as he had always done.

Daniel's enemies, the other supervisors and governors, were watching out for this to happen, just as they had planned, and they immediately reported that they had seen Daniel praying to God and that he had, therefore, broken the new law.

The king was most upset when he heard this, and did his best to find some way to rescue Daniel. He looked for a solution all day. He kept trying until sunset when the supervisors and governors returned for the king's verdict.

'Your Majesty, you know that according to the laws of our land that no order which the king issues can be changed,' the spokesman declared. King Darius knew this to be true, so, with a heavy heart he gave orders for Daniel to be arrested. Daniel was thrown into the pit containing hungry lions. King Darius called to Daniel in the pit, 'I hope that your God, who you serve loyally, will save you.'

A huge stone was put over the mouth of the pit, and the king placed his royal seal on the stone, so that no one could rescue Daniel. Then the king returned to his rooms in the palace unable to sleep or eat and sick with worry.

Very early the following morning King Darius hurried to the pit. He called out anxiously, 'Daniel, you are a good servant to the living God! Did your God save you from the lions?'

Then King Darius heard Daniel answer, 'May Your Majesty live for ever! God sent his angel to shut the mouths of the lions so that they could not harm me. God knew that I was innocent and that I have done nothing wrong to you, your Majesty.'

The king was overjoyed to hear Daniel's voice, and he immediately gave orders for Daniel to be pulled out of the pit. There was not a single mark on him and he was completely safe. The king was furious with his supervisors and governors who had plotted so deviously, so he gave orders to have them, their wives and children, thrown into the pit of lions.

An angel visits Mary

Mary was a girl who lived in a town called Galilee. She was engaged to be married to a man called Joseph who was a descendant of the great Jewish king called David. One day God sent an angel to Mary. The angel was called Gabriel, and he had a message for her from God. The angel spoke to Mary and told her that God was with her and that she was blessed.

Mary was terrified by the angel and his words. What on earth could he mean? 'Don't be frightened, Mary,' the angel continued. 'You will give birth to a son, and you will call him Jesus. He will grow up to be great and he will be called the Son of the Most High God. God will make him a king and his kingdom will go on for ever!'

John the Baptist baptises Jesus

John was a preacher and he was Jesus's cousin. He spoke to many people urging them to turn away from all their wrongdoings, and he told the people that God would forgive their sins. Crowds of people came to hear John speak, and he would baptise them by taking them into the river as a sign that God had washed away and forgiven their sins

Jesus, John's cousin, also came to John to be baptised. While Jesus was praying, the Holy Spirit, like a dove, came down from Heaven onto Jesus. Then a voice was heard from heaven, 'You are my own dear Son. I am pleased with you.'

Jesus appears to his disciples after his death

It was late one Sunday evening, and Jesus's disciples had gathered together in a locked room. Jesus had just been arrested, crucified and had died, and they were afraid that the Jewish authorities might seek them out and punish them too.

Suddenly, Jesus came and stood with them in the room. 'May peace be with you,' he said, and then he showed them the nail wounds in his hands and the cut in his side. The disciples were overjoyed at seeing Jesus, their friend and leader. He was alive again.

Then Jesus spoke to them. 'My Father sent me, and so I am sending you,' he said. He breathed on them and said, 'You are receiving the Holy Spirit. If you forgive people's sins, then they are forgiven but if you do not forgive them, they are not forgiven.'

> ### *The coming of the Holy Spirit*
>
> After Jesus had died many of his followers met together in a house. Suddenly, from the sky came a noise which sounded like a strong wind blowing and the noise filled the whole building. Then, as they looked around, they saw what appeared to be tongues of fire which spread out and touched each person. Everyone there was filled with the Holy Spirit and they all began to talk in different languages. The Holy Spirit had given them the power to do this.

Step 3 Evaluate

What is the value of the Christian views of God for Christians?

- Pupils prepare questions to ask a Christian visitor. Discuss as a class which questions are useful and appropriate, for example:
  - How do you like to describe the God you believe in?
  - Are there other descriptions of God that you find useful, helpful or meaningful?
  - How do descriptions of God help you?
  - Have you always believed that God is like that description, or have your ideas changed? Why?
  - Are there any stories or images of God that have helped you with your description of God?
- Pupils could use their questions to ask a Christian friend or relative (as homework), or arrange e-mail correspondents from a local church congregation if possible. The class should discuss the answers they receive.
- Pupils complete the speech bubble worksheet (see artwork 2 on the CD). Discuss as a class. ◀

> ### Questions to prompt discussion
>
> - What do you think Christians might consider is the most important thing about God? What do they value about God?
> - Do all Christians have the same views of God, do you think?
> - Do all Christians believe in the existence of God, do you think?
> - Why do you think that some people believe in God and others do not?

Step 4 Communicate

What are our responses to the concept of God?

- Produce sets of cards (see Figure 3.4 and the CD). In small groups of three or four the ◀ pupils should arrange the cards in order of priority.
- Pupils will need time in their groups to discuss each card and decide where it should be placed. They may find that they have to create an alternative pattern because they cannot agree on where to place cards. The point of the exercise is to encourage discussion.

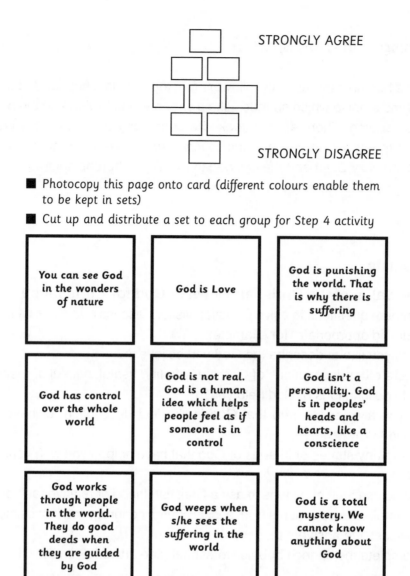

STRONGLY AGREE

STRONGLY DISAGREE

- Photocopy this page onto card (different colours enable them to be kept in sets)
- Cut up and distribute a set to each group for Step 4 activity

You can see God in the wonders of nature	God is Love	God is punishing the world. That is why there is suffering
God has control over the whole world	God is not real. God is a human idea which helps people feel as if someone is in control	God isn't a personality. God is in peoples' heads and hearts, like a conscience
God works through people in the world. They do good deeds when they are guided by God	God weeps when s/he sees the suffering in the world	God is a total mystery. We cannot know anything about God

Figure 3.4

- Prepare for a class debate. Pupils should prepare arguments for and against the motion on the writing frame (see Figure 3.5 and the CD) in preparation for the debate. Suggested motions:

1 'Belief in God helps people to live happier lives.'
2 'There is a God who controls the universe.'
3 'God was created by human beings.'
4 'People should be taught to believe in God.'

Or pupils could decide their own motion as a class.

CLASS DEBATE

The motion for debate is: ....

....

....

Arguments for the motion	Arguments against the motion

● Decide if you agree with the statement (the motion for debate). If you do agree you are for the motion, if you disagree you are against the motion.

● Prepare the points you want to make in the debate which will persuade the rest of the class to agree with you.

● Consider what people who disagree with you might say and jot down those points so that you are prepared to argue against them.

Figure 3.5

Step 5 Apply

How do views about God apply to pupils' own and other's lives?

● Pupils discuss in pairs where they have heard ideas about God, and list them. The teacher should collate the lists for discussion. Create a bar chart, perhaps, showing how often each source has been mentioned.

Questions to prompt discussion

● What is the most common source for hearing about God in the class?
● Which is the least common source?
● Do you think that would be true in every class?
● Do you think that would be the same picture in other schools in the area?
● Can you think of other areas or communities which might have a different pattern? Why might that be?
● Why do you think some people believe in a God and others do not?

- Pupils, individually or in pairs, consider the different situations on the chart provided (see CD and Figure 3.6). They should mark in which situation they feel that they personally would be most likely to think about a God.
- Using another colour, they might speculate and mark in what situations or circumstances they think others might be most likely to think about a God.
- Compare charts and discuss differences and similarities.
- Some pupils might think of different circumstances to add to the list.

Questions to prompt discussion

- Are some situations more likely to make people think about a God than others? Why? Why not?
- Can people create situations that make them think about a God (such as a place of worship)?
- Does thinking about a God always make people feel safe? In what situation might thinking about a God make someone feel unsafe (perhaps following natural disasters, if people think of a God as controller of the universe)?

- Pupils produce a written description/explanation of a situation where they or another might think about a God, and also when thinking about a God might feel threatening.

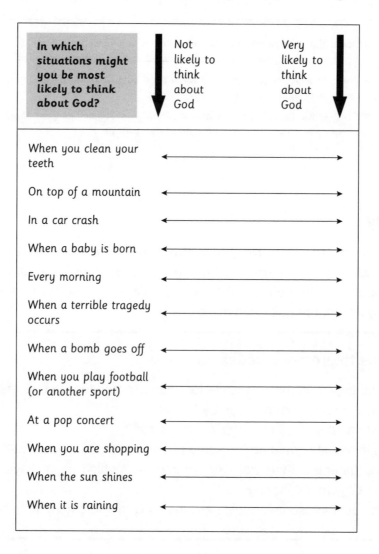

In which situations might you be most likely to think about God?	Not likely to think about God	Very likely to think about God
When you clean your teeth	←――――――――――――――→	
On top of a mountain	←――――――――――――――→	
In a car crash	←――――――――――――――→	
When a baby is born	←――――――――――――――→	
Every morning	←――――――――――――――→	
When a terrible tragedy occurs	←――――――――――――――→	
When a bomb goes off	←――――――――――――――→	
When you play football (or another sport)	←――――――――――――――→	
At a pop concert	←――――――――――――――→	
When you are shopping	←――――――――――――――→	
When the sun shines	←――――――――――――――→	
When it is raining	←――――――――――――――→	

Figure 3.6

The Hindu view of God

Step 2 **Contextualise**

What are the Hindu views of God?

The teacher should lead pupils through Step 1 before engaging with Steps 2 and 3, then return to Steps 4 and 5 in the book (pages 35–38) to effectively complete the enquiry into the concept of God.

- Pupils consider someone close to them (mum, dad, brother, granny, friend) and draw a quick sketch of him or her showing something he or she is good at, or a dimension of his or her character/personality, for example:
  ○ Dad is good at cooking. Draw dad in a chef's hat holding a frying pan.
  ○ Granny is very generous. Draw granny sprinkling coins.
- Discuss ideas with the class before they start, and allow only five minutes' drawing time. Pupils then draw the same person showing something else he or she is good at, or another dimension of his or her personality. Repeat a third time.
- Display and discuss the results.

> **Questions to prompt discussion**
>
> - What can you tell about this person from these three pictures?
> - Is this an effective way of expressing ideas about someone? Why? Why not?

- Pupils work in groups. Distribute a murti (devotional model) or a poster of a Hindu deity to each group (see CD for images Figure 3.7 artwork 3). Pupils should discuss and note what attributes or personality this character has, or what particular skills he or she has. Pupils share their ideas with the rest of the class.

Note that many Hindus believe in **one God** (Brahman), but in many different forms to show the many different characteristics and attributes of Brahman. Relate this concept to the pupil's drawings of a relative or friend.

- Through the stories and images provided below (and on the CD) pupils explore characteristics associated with Hindu deities.
- Pupils should produce pamphlets which could be used at a Hindu temple explaining to visitors the Hindu view of God expressed in the stories and images of them.

The power of the Goddess Durga

The Gods all lived in heaven and were ruling there. The demons, however, who lived on the earth, were very unhappy. 'We used to rule in heaven,' they complained, 'until the Gods came and took over.' The demons were furious and wanted heaven back again.

They decided to go to the wicked and powerful demon called Mahish. He was so cruel and mischievous that everyone was terrified of him. Years before he had been granted special powers so that no man could ever kill him. Only a woman would ever be able to kill Mahish. He was very pleased to be approached by all the demons, and before long he had gathered together a huge and terrifying army to attack the Gods in heaven.

The battle commenced. The Gods fought bravely and endured violence and suffering for a hundred years, but in the end they were forced out of heaven. The wicked Mahish had won and became the new king of heaven.

The Gods were devastated. What could they do to win back heaven and rid the world of the wicked Mahish? They concentrated their thoughts and all their powers together to seek help. Gradually a light began to shine and it became brighter and brighter, like the sun, and out of the light appeared a terrifying sight. A powerful Goddess emerged riding on a savage lion. She was the wonderful Goddess Durga.

The Gods gave Durga all their most dangerous weapons, and off she rode to challenge the wicked Mahish. Mahish was so powerful and he had such a strong army that he had no fear of Durga. The demon army charged her from all sides. However, they could not harm her. The ferocious lion on which she rode killed them all with his powerful jaws.

Now there was only Mahish left. He was quick thinking and instantly changed himself into a gigantic buffalo which thundered around uprooting mountains and making the ground quake. Durga tried to capture him with a rope, but he changed to a lion and freed himself. In his efforts to avoid Durga's attacks he changed into a man, then an elephant and then a buffalo again. This time Durga stamped on him with her foot so that he was unable to move, and as quick as a flash, she swung her sword into the air and cut off his head just at the point when he turned himself back into his demon form. A woman had killed Mahish.

The Gods were overjoyed that the earth and heaven were now rid of the most wicked demon. The world was restored to peace once more.

The kindness of Lord Krishna

When Krishna was young he was strong and brave. He was clever, he could play beautiful music and he loved having fun. Krishna had a very good friend who was not so lucky. He was not strong like Krishna because he was not very well, but he and Krishna loved to play together, and they laughed and joked constantly.

Years later, when Krishna was a man, he became ruler of the land. He lived in a great palace with many servants and everything that he could wish for. His old friend, however, was very poor. He could not work because of his illness, and he and his wife lived in a small shack and they were always short of food.

'Why don't you go and see your old friend Krishna?' suggested the poor man's wife one day. 'He might help us.' The poor man agreed, but wondered what he could take as a gift to such a fine ruler. He had nothing except a little rice, so this he took in a small cloth as a gift.

When the poor man arrived at the palace gates and asked to see Lord Krishna the palace guards laughed at him. How could such a poor, weak man be allowed to visit the great ruler Lord Krishna?

Luckily, Krishna was nearby. He heard the familiar voice of his old friend, and rushed to the palace gates to welcome him in. What a wonderful time they had remembering their old pranks and laughing and joking together, just as they had done when they were boys. Time passed really quickly and soon it was time for the poor man to leave. Krishna bid him a safe journey, and off went the poor man on the road back home with a smile on his face and a happy heart full of good memories.

As he was nearly home he realised how silly he had been. The poor man had forgotten to give Krishna his gift of rice, and even worse, he had forgotten to ask for help. Just then the man's wife came running out to meet him. She was smiling and waving. 'A wonderful thing has happened,' she said. 'Our shack has gone and in its place is a sturdy house and all the store rooms are filled with food!' The poor man was amazed. His old friend Krishna had shown such love and kindness without ever being asked.

Questions to prompt discussion

- What can we know about some Hindu views of God from this story/image?
- Does anything in this story/image surprise you?
- Is God different in the different stories/images? In what way?

Step 3 Evaluate

What is the value of the Hindu views of God for Hindus?

- The pupils should prepare questions to ask a Hindu visitor. Discuss as a class which questions are useful and appropriate, for example:
  - How do you like to describe the God you believe in?
  - Are there other descriptions of God that you find useful, helpful or meaningful?
  - How do descriptions of God help you?
  - Have you always believed that God is like that description, or have your ideas changed? Why?
  - Are there any stories or images of God that have helped you with your description of God?
- Arrange to contact members of a Hindu community as e-mail correspondents if possible, so pupils can ask them their questions. Discuss the answers the pupils receive.
- Pupils complete the speech bubble worksheet (see the CD artwork 4).
- Discuss as a class using the prompts below.

Questions to prompt discussion

- What do you think Hindus might consider is the most important thing about their view of God? What do they value about God?
- Do all Hindus have the same views of God, do you think?
- Do all Hindus believe in the existence of God, do you think?
- Why do you think that some people believe in God and others do not?

Return to Steps 4 and 5 on pages 36–38 of the book to complete the cycle of learning.

The Jewish view of God

The teacher should lead pupils through Step 1 before engaging with Steps 2 and 3 provided here, then return to Steps 4 and 5 in the book (pages 35–38) to effectively complete the enquiry into the concept of God.

Step 2 Contextualise

What are the Jewish ideas about God?

- Pupils individually or in groups investigate the Jewish stories provided below (and on the CD) and remembered during Jewish festival times, which illustrate some of God's characteristics. Different groups could each take a different story to report back to the rest of the class.
- Pupils should record features of the story and note how God could be described in the story to report back in class discussion. What is God like in the stories?

The story of Hannukah

The Jews lived in Israel but their land had been invaded by the Syrians. During the Syrian occupation an emperor called Antiochus came to power. He worshipped Greek gods and wanted to impose his beliefs on all the Jews in his empire. He built statues of the Greek gods and tried to make the Jews worship them. He even tried to make them worship him. Pigs were sacrificed in the Jewish temple and statues erected in the holiest part of the temple.

The Jews could stand it no longer. A Jewish revolt broke out. Some Jews, led by a man called Mattathias and later his son, Judah the Maccabbee, escaped into the hills and started to fight back against the Syrians. They persisted in their fighting for a long time until eventually the Syrian army retreated. The Jews were able to enter their temple once more. They tore down the offending statues and scrubbed the temple clean, and rededicated it once more to God.

They needed to light the oil lamp to show God's blessing of the temple, but only a small amount of oil could be found. It would only last for one day – but a great miracle happened. God made the oil last, not for one day, but for eight whole days until more oil had been found and prepared.

A story remembered at Shavuot

The Jewish people were nomadic. Led by Moses, they lived in the desert and were guided and cared for by God. The Jews were camped by Mount Sinai, and one day God told Moses that all his people should be prepared. After three days the mountain began to tremble and ash, smoke and flames shot out of the mountain.

Moses went up the mountain to speak to God and all the Jewish people waited, terrified. After 40 days Moses returned, covered in ash and dirt, but carrying two great slabs of stone. On the stones were written special laws from God. God had shown his people how to live and provided all the guidance they needed. They would keep these laws for ever and remember that the laws came from God because he cares for his people.

The story remembered at Pesach

Way back in the history of the Jews, the Jewish people lived in Egypt and were slaves to the Egyptians. But God was looking after his people. One day God spoke to Moses and told him to lead the Jews out of Egypt to freedom.

Moses pleaded with the pharaoh of Egypt many times, but he refused to let the Jewish slaves go free. So God sent plagues on the Egyptian people. The river Nile turned to blood, swarms of frogs, gnats and flies plagued the Egyptian homes, a disease killed all the cattle, the Egyptians developed boils, there were storms and hailstones, locusts ate all the plants, then there was darkness and all the first-born Egyptian children died.

This last plague was too much for the pharaoh, who told Moses to leave with all the Jewish slaves. That night they escaped and made their way across the desert to the Red Sea. When they looked back they could see that they were being pursued by the Egyptian army. But God helped the Jews. The Red Sea parted and they were able to walk across to the other side. When the sea returned it drowned the Egyptians who were pursuing the Jews. God had saved his people and guided them to freedom.

- Pupils present their findings to the class, focusing on appropriate descriptions for God in the story.

Questions to prompt discussion

- Do you think this group of pupils has used appropriate descriptions for the way God is in this story?
- Can you think of any other descriptions for God in this story?
- Why do you think festival stories are important to Jewish people?

- Duplicate and distribute copies of the Shema, a Jewish prayer, (see CD and Figure 3.8) to pupils and ask them to highlight any further descriptions of God.

The Shema

Hear O Israel: The Lord our G-d is one Lord;
and you shall love the Lord your G-d
with all your heart,
and with all your soul,
and with all your might.
and these words which I command you this day
shall be upon your heart,
and you shall teach them diligently to your children,
and shall talk of them when you sit in your house,
and when you walk by the way,
and when you lie down, and when you rise.

Deuteronomy Chapter 6 verse 4-7

Figure 3.8

> **Questions to prompt discussion**
>
> - What does the Shema tell you about the Jewish view of God?
> - How important do you think the Shema is to Jews? Why?
> - Can you think of reasons why some devout Jews do not create pictures of God or write God's name?

Step 3 Evaluate

What is the value of the Jewish views of God for Jews?

- Pupils prepare questions to ask a Jewish visitor. Discuss as a class which questions are useful and appropriate, such as:
  - How do you like to describe the God you believe in?
  - Are there other descriptions of God that you find useful, helpful or meaningful?
  - How do descriptions of God help you?
  - Have you always believed that God is like that description, or have your ideas changed? Why?
  - Are there any stories of God that have helped you with your description of God?
- Arrange to contact members of a Jewish community if possible perhaps as e-mail correspondents, so pupils can ask them their questions. Discuss the answers the pupils receive.
- Pupils complete the speech bubble worksheet (see CD artwork 5).
- Discuss as a class using the prompts below

> **Questions to prompt discussion**
>
> - What do you think Jews might consider is the most important thing about their view of God? What do they value about God?
> - Do all Jews think the same do you think?
> - Do you think all Jews believe in the existence of God?
> - Why do you think some people believe in the existence of God, and others do not?

Return to Steps 4 and 5 on pages 35–38 of the book to complete the cycle of learning.

The Muslim view of God

Step 2 Contextualise

What are the Muslim views of God?

The teacher should lead pupils through Step 1 before engaging with Steps 2 and 3, then return to Steps 4 and 5 in the book (pages 35–38) to effectively complete the enquiry into the concept of God.

- Pupils consider someone they know well (brother, granny, mum, dad, friend), and think of as many words to describe them as possible (for instance, Josh the nimble, the crafty, the generous, the forgiving, the amusing).
- Pupils share their ideas with the class.

Questions to prompt discussion

- Are these helpful descriptions?
- Do they help us know about the person?
- Are some people easier to describe than others? Why? Why not?

- Show the pupils the 99 names of Allah (see CD artwork 6). ◀
- Pupils highlight or note any of these names that they find surprising, or that they do not understand, and discuss them as a class.
- Show the picture (see CD artwork 7) of a Muslim reciting the 99 names of Allah (God) ◀ with the help of prayer beads. Pupils speculate about why they think reciting the names of Allah is important to Muslims. (There are no images of Allah in Islam.)
- Pupils in small groups speculate about why there are no images within Islam, then share their ideas as a class.
- Show the comments from Muslims below (available on CD Figure 3.8B). Did pupils' ◀ suggestions match up with the comments from Muslims?

Wazim is 14. He says:
Allah is so powerful, so great, so wonderful that us human beings couldn't possibly imagine what he is like.

Kadija is 12. She says:
I could never try to draw a picture of Allah (God) because to reduce someone so big and powerful to a simple picture would be like an insult.

Lamin is 15. He says:
Images, statues or pictures of Allah would give the wrong impression. Allah is far greater than any human being could show. Our religion requires us to keep Allah in our minds. We might be distracted by statues or pictures and some people might start to worship the statue instead of Allah.

Abdul is 10. He says:
Saying all the 99 names for Allah helps me remember how wonderful he is. If I say the names I know I am concentrating on Allah during that time. I am trying to learn all the 99 names but I do not know them all yet.

The Imam in the mosque explains:
In the mosque there are no pictures or statues of Allah or any humans or animals. Muslims believe that these might distract worshippers, and Islam is strictly against idol worship. During worship it is important to concentrate on the greatness of Allah. In the mosque classroom where Muslim children come to learn to read the Qur'an, there are many books. None of them have pictures of Allah, Muhammad or any other prophets. No artist could show them accurately. Pupils learn to say the 99 names of Allah so that they can concentrate on his greatness.

Figure 3.8B

Step 3 Evaluate

What is the value of the Muslim views of God for Muslims?

- Pupils prepare questions to ask a Muslim visitor. Discuss as a class which questions are useful and appropriate, for example:
  - How do you like to describe the God you believe in?
  - Are there other descriptions of God that you find useful, helpful or meaningful?
  - How do descriptions of God help you?
  - Have you always believed that God is like that description, or have your ideas changed? Why?
  - Are there any stories or teachings that have helped you with your description of God?
- Arrange to contact members of a Muslim community if possible, perhaps as e-mail correspondents, so pupils can ask them their questions. Discuss the answers the pupils receive.
- ▶ Pupils complete a speech bubble worksheet (see CD artwork 8).
- Discuss as a class using the prompts below.

> #### Questions to prompt discussion
>
> - What do you think Muslims might consider is the most important thing about their view of God? What do they value about God?
> - Do all Muslims think the same, do you think?
> - Do you think all Muslims believe in the existence of God?
> - Why do you think some people believe in the existence of God, and others do not?

Return to Steps 4 and 5 on pages 35–38 of the book to complete the cycle of learning.

The Sikh view of God

Step 2 Contextualise

What are the Sikh ideas about God?

The teacher should lead pupils through Step 1 before engaging with Steps 2 and 3, then return to Steps 4 and 5 in the book (pages 35–38) to effectively complete the enquiry into the concept of God.

- ▶ Duplicate and distribute copies of the Mool Mantra (see CD and Figure 3.9).
- ▶ Pupils discuss each line and speculate on what it means. They should then complete the task (see CD Figure 3.9) of matching phrases to the Mool Mantra. Duplicate and cut up the cards for the task.

Mool Mantra

There is one God	There is only one God
Eternal Truth is God's name	God's name will go on God is true
Creator of all things and the pervading spirit	God created everything and God's spirit is in everything
Fearless and without hatred	God is frightened of nothing and hates nothing
Timeless and formless	God has always existed and will always exist. God has no body, shape or form
Beyond birth and death	God can never be born and will never die
Self enlightened	God knows all things
By the grace of the Guru God is known	People can know about God through the Gurus

Figure 3.9

Questions to prompt discussion

- Which do you think is the most important statement for Sikhs? Why?
- Why do you think Sikhs do not have images of God?
- Why do you think Sikhs recite this prayer every day?
- Do you think reciting this prayer makes a difference to the way they behave and what they do? Why? Why not?

Step 3 Evaluate

What is the value of the Sikh views of God for Sikhs?

- Pupils prepare questions to ask a Sikh visitor. Discuss as a class which questions are useful and appropriate, for example:
  - How do you like to describe the God you believe in?
  - Are there other descriptions of God that you find useful, helpful or meaningful?
  - How do descriptions of God help you?

- ○ Have you always believed that God is like that description or have your ideas changed? Why?
- ○ Are there any stories or teachings that have helped you with your view of God?
- Arrange to contact members of a Sikh community, perhaps as e-mail correspondents, so pupils can ask them their questions. Discuss the answers the pupils receive.
- Pupils complete a speech bubble worksheet (see CD artwork 9).
- Discuss as a class using the prompts below.

Questions to prompt discussion

- What do you think Sikhs might consider is the most important thing about their view of God? What do they value about God?
- Do all Sikhs think the same, do you think?
- Do you think all Sikhs believe in the existence of God?
- Why do you think some people believe in the existence of God and others do not?

Return to Steps 4 and 5 on pages 35–38 in the book to complete the cycle of learning.

Resources on the CD

Figures

3.2 a and b – Hymns and prayers about the Christian view of the nature of God
3.3   Cards to sort
3.4   Cards – responses to the concept of God
3.5   Writing frame – motion for debate
3.6   Chart – thinking about a God
3.7   Artwork – six Hindu deities
3.8   The Shema – a Jewish prayer
3.8B Comments from Muslims
3.9   Mool Mantra

Artwork

2.   Christian speaker
4.   Hindu speaker
5.   Jewish speaker
6.   The 99 names of Allah
7.   A Muslim reciting the 99 names of Allah
8.   Muslim speaker
9.   Sikh speaker

Stories: Christian

God calls to Moses from a burning bush
God protects Daniel in the pit of lions
An Angel visits Mary

John the Baptist baptises Jesus
Jesus appears to his disciples after his death
The coming of the Holy Spirit

Stories: Hindu

The power of the Goddess Durga
The kindness of Lord Krishna

Stories: Jewish

The story of Hannukah
A story remembered at Shavuot
The story remembered at Pesach

Concept: *holy*

For many pupils the concept of *holy* is one that they may not have considered or encountered very often. The concept is fundamentally important, however, to enable pupils to develop some understanding about religion and how many religious people view and respond to certain objects or people. The book provides the example of Mary who, for many Christians, is regarded as *holy*, being chosen by God to give birth to God on earth (or God's son). This unit, therefore, is particularly successful in the autumn term in the run-up to Christmas. It also uses the imagery and traditions of the Catholic Church which explicitly depicts and describes Mary as *holy*. There is also the example of the Torah scrolls as *holy* for Jewish people. In both these units it is necessary to use religious material in the **enquire** element of the cycle in order to illustrate the meaning of *holy*.

Christian beliefs in Holy Mary, mother of God
The Torah Scrolls, holy for Jews

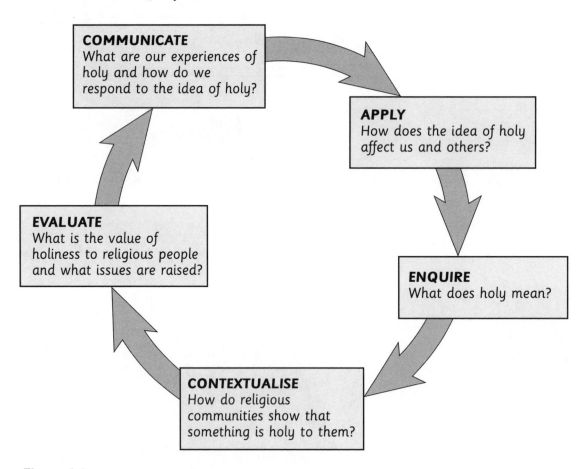

COMMUNICATE
What are our experiences of holy and how do we respond to the idea of holy?

APPLY
How does the idea of holy affect us and others?

ENQUIRE
What does holy mean?

CONTEXTUALISE
How do religious communities show that something is holy to them?

EVALUATE
What is the value of holiness to religious people and what issues are raised?

Figure 4.1

Christian beliefs in Holy Mary, mother of God

Step 1 Enquire

What does *holy* mean?

- Show pupils the image of Mary (provided on CD: see artwork 1). The pupils should speculate about who it is and what they notice about the image.

> ### Questions to prompt discussion
>
> - How does she look?
> - What does she think of the baby?
> - Why do you think that?
> - Where would you find it?
> - Who would use it?
> - What for?
> - How do other people feel about it?

- The pupils should draw a picture or make a clay model of Mary and write a label saying 'I think that this is ...'.
- Tell the story of Mary being visited by the angel Gabriel (below and on CD).

Mary is visited by an angel

There was a town called Nazareth and one day God sent an angel, called Gabriel, with a special message to this town. The message was for a girl called Mary who was engaged to a man called Joseph. They were planning to get married.

The angel Gabriel suddenly appeared to Mary. Mary was terrified. Then the angel spoke to Mary. 'Peace be with you. God is with you. God has blessed you.' Mary was shaking with fright. She wondered what was happening and what the angel meant. Then the angel spoke again. 'Don't be afraid, Mary. God has been good to you. You will become pregnant and you will have a baby boy and you will call him Jesus. The baby will become great and will be called the son of the most high God. God will make him a king.'

Mary then answered the angel. She could not understand what she was being told. 'How can this happen? I am not married. I am a virgin.' The angel Gabriel spoke again. 'The Holy Spirit and God's power will rest on you. That is why your son will be called the son of God. There is nothing that God cannot do.'

Mary then answered the angel. 'I am God's servant,' she said. 'May things happen as you have said.' Then the angel Gabriel left.

Questions to prompt discussion

- Where do pupils think the angel was from in the story?
- Why is there an angel in the story?
- Could the message from the angel have been sent to Mary any other way?
- Would that have been as effective (or seemed so special) in the story?
- What is the most important thing that the angel said, do you think?
- How do you think Mary felt?

- ▶ Pupils should look at artists' impressions of this story (the Annunciation) (see artwork 2 on CD). How does the artist show that Mary is *holy* and chosen by God? Discuss. Would pupils want to add things to their original pictures/clay models to show that Mary is holy?
- Pupils should discuss with partners what they think *holy* means. Can they decide on a description which could be used in a 'glossary of terms' or a dictionary definition?
- ▶ Pupils should complete the writing frame (see Figure 4.2 and CD) with a definition or description of *holy.*

Holy means ......

Figure 4.2

Step 2 Contextualise

How do Christians show that they believe Mary is *holy*?

- Distribute to pupils copies of carols which identify Mary as *holy*, Mother of God, blessed and so on. Pupils highlight phrases and descriptions of Mary. Collate pupils' ideas in class discussion.

Questions to prompt discussion

- Which descriptions of Mary point to her being *holy*?
- Which words or phrases do you think are the best to describe *holiness*?
- Do all the descriptions give the impression that Mary is *holy*?

- Investigate the 'Hail Mary' prayer (supplied on CD Fig 4.3A). Pupils prepare questions ◀ to ask a Catholic visitor about their feelings and ideas about Mary. When do Catholics show reverence or pray to Mary? Why? What happens?
- Visit a Catholic church (or a website) which shows a Lady Chapel, and/or a stained glass window, and/or other images and icons of Mary. Pupils should take digital pictures or draw pictures. Pupils should ask the priest or investigate how and why the images and icons are used by believers.

Step 3 Evaluate

What is the value of the *holiness* of Mary to Christians and what issues are raised?

- Pupils in groups brainstorm all the words they have heard associated with Mary. The teacher should then collate the words and phrases to make a composite list on a whiteboard.
- Pupils individually or in pairs put the words or phrases in order of priority, starting with those they consider to be the most helpful for some Christians to show Mary's *holiness*, and ending with the least helpful.
- Lead a class discussion about the value of Mary's *holiness* to some Christians.

Questions to prompt discussion

- Would it matter if some Christians thought Mary was very ordinary and not *holy* at all?
- Why? Why not?
- Would there be images and icons of Mary if Christians did not think she was *holy*?
- Do the images and icons of Mary help Christians to think about Mary being *holy*?
- How do the images of Mary help some Christians, do you think?

- Create a 'conscience alley' for children to pass through. The pupils should stand in two lines facing each other, leaving a pathway (alley) down the middle. All the pupils on one side try to persuade the pupil walking through the 'alley' that Mary is very holy, using persuasive arguments. The pupils opposite them try to persuade the pupil walking the alley that Mary was just an ordinary girl, also using persuasive arguments. Pupils need to whisper their comments to avoid mayhem! Several pupils can walk the alley and share their feelings and opinions at the end.

Step 4 Communicate

What are our experiences of *holy* and how do we respond to the idea of *holy*?

- Allow time for quiet reflection, and perhaps play quiet music. Ask pupils to sit quietly and consider people or things that they would/might describe as *holy* in their own experience. What other word might they use if *holy* is not right for them?
- Pupils draw a picture and write a few words or a description of their ideas. What would they include in the picture to show other people they think this person or object is *holy* (or otherwise)?

● Invite pupils to share responses. Encourage pupils to explain why they consider someone or something to be *holy* for themselves or others. What qualities does it have, or what memories are evoked?

Questions to prompt discussion

● Do you think the person/object you have chosen is *holy*? Why? Why not?
● Does it match up to the descriptions and definitions we wrote in Step 2?
● What makes it *holy* (or not *holy*)?
● What do other class members think?
● Is it *holy* in the same way that Mary is *holy* for some Christians?
● Why? Why not?

Step 5 Apply

How does the idea of *holy* affect us and others?

● Pupils consider when they or others think about their *holy* (or precious, treasured, special) person. How do they feel? What difference does it make?
● Pupils then consider when they think about a *holy* (or precious, treasured, special) object. Is the object a reminder of someone or an event? Does thinking about it or handling it help them? How? Why?
● In pairs pupils discuss how they or others use their objects, where they keep them, and how often they look at or handle them.

The Torah scrolls, *holy* for Jews

Step 1 Enquire

What does *holy* mean?

● Show pupils the image of the Torah scrolls provided (on CD: see artwork 3). Pupils speculate about what they are and what they notice about the image.

Questions to prompt discussion

● Where would you find them, do you think?
● Who would use them?
● What for?
● How do other people feel about them?
● How do you think that they might be treated?

● Tell the story of Moses receiving the commandments from God (see below and CD).

God's laws are given to his people

God's chosen people were the Jews. He had helped them escape from slavery in Egypt and, led by Moses, they were now in the desert. They were safe at last and they were free to worship God. The Jews were a nomadic people and wandered the desert, setting up camps and living off the land, with God's help.

At one time the Jews were camped by a mountain called Sinai. Moses went up the mountain to pray, and when he was there God spoke to him. 'You know that I have chosen the Jews as my special people,' God said. 'They must be dedicated to me, obey me and serve me like priests.'

Moses told the Jews what God had said and they answered happily, 'We will do everything that our God asks.'

God had more instructions for his people. He spoke to Moses again. 'Tell the people that they must wash themselves and their clothes and purify themselves. In two days I will show myself to my people.'

The Jewish people purified themselves as they had been instructed and were ready for God. On the third day there was smoke around the mountain. There was terrifying thunder and lightning and a thunderous trumpet blast was heard. The people were frightened and trembling as they followed Moses out of the camp towards the foot of the mountain. The mountain began to quake, fire could be seen at the top of the mountain and smoke swirled around, and the noise of the trumpet blast became louder and louder. Moses spoke to God and God answered him in a voice of thunder. The people were terrified.

Moses went up the mountain. When he returned he told all the Jewish people all that God had commanded and they declared, 'We will obey God's laws and do everything that he says.'

God's laws were on two huge pieces of stone, and God gave Moses careful instructions about where to keep his laws. They were to be placed in a special wooden box lined and covered in gold with golden winged creatures on the lid. God's laws were to be kept holy in a special tent. The tent was made following God's careful instructions and was anointed with sacred oils and dedicated to God.

Now the Jewish people had God's laws with them. They could remember their agreement with God and keep his laws holy. God's presence was with them at all times.

Questions to prompt discussion

- Which part of the story do you think might be most significant for Jews? Why?
- Is it important that God features in the story, do you think? Why? Why not?
- The story says that God's laws should be 'kept *holy*' by the Jews. What does that mean, do you think?
- Can anything be 'kept *holy*' do you think? Why/Why not?

- The pupils complete the writing frame (see Figure 4.3 and CD).

To "keep holy" means ......

Figure 4.3

Step 2 Contextualise

How do Jews show that they believe the Torah is holy?

- Show the pupils the pictures of the Torah scrolls in the Ark (supplied on CD: see artwork 4) which contain all God's laws. Draw their attention again to the silver ornaments on the scrolls and the velvet or silver covers.
- Visit a synagogue if possible, and ask if the scrolls can be 'undressed' and opened for pupils to see the Hebrew writing and the use of the yad.
- Pupils explore how copies of the Torah are written (or ask during the synagogue visit).
- Pupils explore (through websites or books) the Simchat Torah celebrations (see the illustration supplied on CD as artwork 5).
- Pupils in pairs or groups should list the things that Jews do to keep the Torah holy.
- Pupils complete the writing frame provided (see Figure 4.4 and CD).

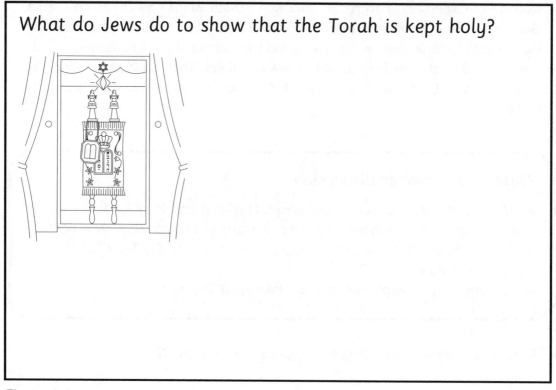

What do Jews do to show that the Torah is kept holy?

Figure 4.4

Step 3 Evaluate

What is the value of the *holiness* of the Torah to Jews, and what issues are raised?

- Set up a role play situation with the pupils working in groups.

The pupils in role as Jews visit the synagogue on the Sabbath and find that the Torah scrolls have been taken from the Ark and ripped and ruined and thrown on the floor. The silver ornaments have been stolen. Other pupils in role as the police visit the scene of the crime. The police think in terms of the financial cost of replacement. The pupils in role as Jews need to explain to the police the significance of the loss in relation to keeping the Torah holy.

Questions to prompt discussion

- How do you think Jews might feel if this happened?
- Do you think that they would be happy to download all the contents of the Torah from a website and use that instead? Why? Why not?
- What is special about the scrolls to the Jews? Why?
- What would you suggest as a solution to their loss?
- Should they keep their Torah scrolls locked up in a bank in future? Why? Why not?

Go to Steps 4 and 5 in the book (pages 53–54) to complete the cycle of learning.

Resources on the CD

Figures

4.2 A Writing frame – *Holy means*
4.3 Writing frame – *To "keep holy" means*
4.3A Hail Mary prayer
4.4 Writing frame – *What do Jews do to show that the Torah is kept holy?*

Artwork

1. Mary
2a–f. Artists' impressions of the Annunciation
3. The Torah scrolls
4. The Torah scrolls in the Ark
5. Simchat Torah celebrations

Stories: Christian

Mary is visited by an angel

Stories: Jewish

God's laws are given to his people

Concept: *symbol*

This unit of work enables pupils to investigate what *symbols* are and why they are meaningful to individuals and groups of people. Some *symbols* can be elements of the natural world, such as water or fire, while others might be food or items of clothing, and others may be shapes or designs or even gestures. They are *symbols* when they have become imbued with meaning and significance. This unit provides an enquiry into a range of *symbols*. In the book the example of the empty cross is explored as a potent symbol for Christians. This is followed by examples of how the concept *symbol* can be explored within aspects of other major religions.

The *symbol* of the Buddha for Buddhists
The *symbol* of water for Hindus
The *symbol* of Ihram for Muslims
The *symbol* of bread for Jews
The *symbols* of the Kirpan for Sikhs

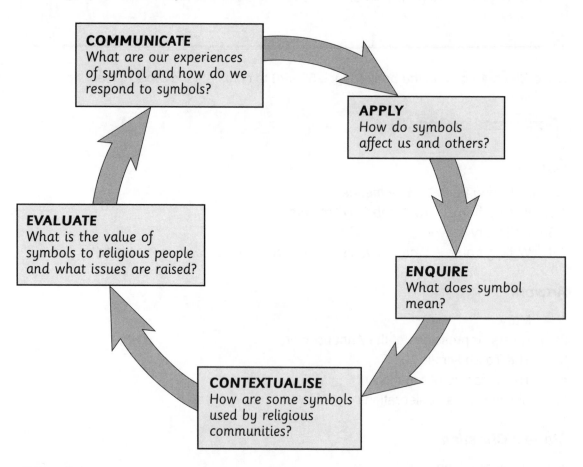

Figure 5.1

The symbol of the empty cross for Christians

Step 1 Enquire

What does *symbol* mean?

- Pupils in pairs look through magazines or newspaper for *symbols* and cut out a few to make a collection.
- Pupil pairs should share with other pairs and interpret each other's symbols.
- The teacher should pose the question, 'Are these signs or *symbols*? What is the difference?' Discuss as a class.
- The teacher should tell pupils the following story and then discuss it.

Sam and his mum and two sisters moved house in the summer. Their old house was on a busy road in a built-up area and it did not have much of a garden, but this new house did. It had a good-sized patch of grass at the back. The trouble was that it was all very bare, and Sam thought it was a bit boring.

A few weeks after they had moved in, Sam's Granddad came to stay. 'Not much going on in this garden, eh, Sam?' was Granddad's comment as Sam showed him around. 'I think we ought to do something about that.' The next day Granddad disappeared to a garden centre and came back with a tree sticking out of the back of the car. It looked pretty spindly but it was very tall and had a huge root ball tied up in a sack. 'You'll need to give me a hand with this, son,' Granddad called to Sam. They planted the tree in the corner of the garden and secured it with a post, then they both stepped back to admire it. 'Not much yet, but it'll soon grow,' Granddad remarked.

That was the last summer that Sam saw Granddad. In the winter Granddad suddenly had a heart attack and never recovered. How sad they all were, but how glad Sam was that they had planted the tree together. Every time he looked at that tree in the garden, Sam thought of his Granddad and the thought filled him with a sad, but warm glow. The tree was a symbol of Granddad's kindness and generosity that would be there in their garden for years and years.

Questions to prompt discussion

- Why did the tree remind Sam of his Granddad?
- Did the tree look like his Granddad?
- Was the tree a sign or a *symbol*?
- What is a s*ymbol*?
- What is a sign?

- Pupils should complete the writing frame (see Figure 5.2 and on CD) with their own definition of a *symbol*.

A symbol is something that.......

Figure 5.2

- The teacher should show the section of the DVD of *The Lion, the Witch and the Wardrobe* that depicts the death of Aslan and his 'resurrection' from the stone table. (She/he might need to provide an overview of the story if pupils are unfamiliar with it.) Pupils should be directed to imagine that they live in Narnia and their beloved leader, Aslan, has been killed by the terrible White Witch, but amazingly, he comes alive again. They want to mark this miraculous event with a *symbol* that could be used every year to help them to remember and celebrate the resurrection of Aslan. What *symbol* could they create to remember when Aslan came alive again?
- Pupils, individually or in pairs, create *symbols* for Narnians. Create a display.
- Pupils should tell members of the class the meaning of their *symbols*, or create labels for the *symbols*.

Step 2 Contextualise

How is the *symbol* of the empty cross used by Christians?

- The teacher should show the pupils artefacts or the pictures of a crucifix and then a plain cross (see those provided on CD as artwork 1a and 1b) and ask them to speculate on what each one symbolises for Christians. What do they think each cross makes Christians think about? What does it remind them of? What does it mean to them?
- Tell the Easter story (see CD).

The Easter story

Jesus was with his followers in a garden. 'Sit here,' he said, 'while I go and pray.' While he was there a crowd of men with clubs and swords arrived to arrest him. They took Jesus to the house of the Jewish high priest where all the elders and chief priests of the Jewish temple were gathered together. They believed that what Jesus had been teaching and preaching to all the people was against the sacred Jewish laws, so they questioned Jesus closely. The chief priests and elders became more and more angry with Jesus. The high priest asked them, 'What do you think?' 'He is guilty and must die!' they answered, and then they started to hit Jesus and spit in his face.

The Jewish elders and chief priests put Jesus in chains, and the next morning they handed him over to the Roman governor. The Roman governor also questioned Jesus, but felt that Jesus had done nothing wrong, so he called to the crowds gathered outside. 'What shall I do with Jesus?' he shouted to them. 'Crucify him!' the crowds shouted back. The crowds were so angry that the Roman governor thought a riot might break out, so he decided to hand Jesus over to Roman soldiers to be taken to be crucified.

Jesus was taken to a hill where crucifixions took place and was nailed to a cross. After many hours of agony Jesus died. That evening a rich man who was a follower of Jesus took Jesus's body. He wrapped it in fresh linen and had it placed in a tomb which had been dug out of the rock. A large stone was placed over the entrance and sealed in place.

On the third day after Jesus had died some women, who had been friends of Jesus, went to visit the tomb. To their amazement the stone had been rolled away from the entrance of the tomb. They rushed inside, but Jesus's body had gone. Inside the tomb was a figure in bright, shining light. 'Jesus is not here,' said the figure. 'He has been raised from death.' The women were thrilled and terrified at the same time. Jesus was alive! They hurried off to tell Jesus's friends and followers. Jesus had died and now he was alive again.

Questions to prompt discussion

- Which parts of this story do you think are most significant for Christians?
- Why?
- Can you think of any *symbols* that Christians use to remind them of the story?
- Which parts of the story do the *symbols* remind Christians about?

- Show the pupils two crosses (a crucifix and a plain cross) and ask them to consider and discuss which parts of the story each cross *symbolises.*
- Visit a church if possible, so pupils can find the use of the two *symbols* in the church. They should take digital pictures for a labelled display in the classroom.

Step 3 Evaluate

What is the value of the *symbol* of the empty cross to Christians and what issues are raised?

- Teachers should duplicate and cut up the cards provided in Figure 5.3 and provide a set for pupils in pairs to sort (see CD Figure 5.3). Pupils in pairs look at the statements, decide which statements a Christian might agree with most, and sort them into order of priority. There are no right or wrong answers here. Pupils should be encouraged to decide for themselves and be able to justify their ideas and share them in class discussion.

Teachers duplicate and cut up the cards and provide a set for each pair of pupils to sort. Which statements might a Christian most strongly agree with? Put in order of priority.
The empty cross is a good basic design and works well in Churches.
The empty cross reminds Christians about Jesus being kind
The empty cross is a reminder of the Easter story
The empty cross is used because the artist could not draw the figure of Jesus
The empty cross reminds Christians that Jesus came alive and is alive for ever
The empty cross is a symbol of God's power to overcome death
The empty cross is used because some people think that the cross with the crucifi ed Jesus looks too gruesome
The empty cross is a powerful symbol that can be found in Christian art, design, cards, books, jewellery and buildings.
The empty cross is so familiar that it has lost its symbolic meaning
The symbol of the empty cross reminds Christians that they too will overcome death, as Jesus did

Figure 5.3

Questions to prompt discussion

- Which do you think might be the most important statement for a Christian?
- Why do you think that?
- Are there any statements that you could discard because they are not appropriate?
- Which are they?
- Why are they not appropriate?
- Do you think there might be other reasons why Christians value the symbol of the empty cross? What are they?
- Do you think there are any similarities between the *symbols* you created for Narnia and the empty cross *symbol*?
- What are the similarities?
- What are the differences?
- What other *symbol* could be used to remind Christians of the resurrection of Jesus?

Step 4 Communicate

What are our experiences of *symbol* and how do we respond to *symbols*?

- Pupils should consider an event in their experience that has particular significance (such as learning to ride a bike, the birth of a new baby brother or sister, or a pet dying) and reflect on the feelings and memories associated with it.
- Pupils create or draw a *symbol* that would serve as a reminder of all those thoughts and feelings.
- Display the results.
- The pupils can talk about their *symbols* in a class discussion.

Questions to prompt discussion

- Does anyone want to comment about any of the *symbols* that they particularly like?
- Why do you like it?
- Does it have meaning for you?
- Can we all know what all the *symbols* mean or are some only understood by the people who created them?
- Does that matter?
- Who are the *symbols* for (the people who made them or everyone else)?

Step 5 Apply

How do *symbols* affect us and others?

- The pupils in groups should brainstorm as many *symbols* as they can think of remembering that *symbols* are not the same as signs,. They might include, for example, birthday candles, football scarves, wedding rings, Easter eggs, the school badge, and any religious symbols they have learned about.
- Collate and discuss the pupils' ideas.

Questions to prompt discussion

- Do we think these are all *symbols*?
- What do they all mean?
- Can we all tell what they all mean? Is that important?
- Which *symbols* are important to you?
- Why? What does it make you think about?
- Do all *symbols* make you feel the same way?
- When do you see these *symbols*?
- Would it matter if there were no *symbols*? Why? Why not?

- Pupils then complete the writing frame shown in Figure 5.4 (also see CD for Figure 5.4).

This symbol is important to me

This symbol is important to me because........

Figure 5.4

The symbol of the Buddha for Buddhists

Pupils should explore Step 1 in the book (page 59) before they engage with Steps 2 and 3 in this section. This should then be followed by Steps 4 and 5 in the book (pages 63–64).

Step 2 Contextualise

How is the *symbol* of the Buddha used by Buddhists?

- Show the pupils the image of the Buddha provided on CD (see artwork 2) and ask them to talk in pairs about what they notice. Discuss as a class,
- Pupils speculate in their pairs what the image might *symbolise*. What does it mean to people and what does it make people think about?
- Compare ideas in discussion.

> ### Questions to prompt discussion
>
> - What do you think this symbol might be used for?
> - Where might you find it?
> - What do you think it might *symbolise* or mean to people?
> - Why do you think that?
> - Out of all the ideas that the class has suggested, do you think there are some ideas that are more likely than others? Why?

- Tell the story of the life of the Buddha (below and on the CD).

The life of the Buddha

Many years ago lived a fine young prince called Siddhartha. He lived in a great palace surrounded by beautiful gardens and forests. His father, the king, loved him dearly and protected him from anything that might upset him. Siddhartha had all that he wanted in life: fine food, beautiful clothes, friends to play with and clever teachers to teach him. He was very happy.

When he grew older he became very curious about life outside the palace. He had never been through the palace gates and he wanted to find out about the world, so one day he arranged for his servant to accompany him on a ride outside the palace grounds. Siddhartha saw four things outside the palace that would change his life entirely.

The first thing he saw was an old man struggling along the road with a stick. He had grey hair and wrinkled skin and he had great difficulty in walking. 'What is wrong with that person?' asked Prince Siddhartha. 'He is old,' replied his servant. 'Everyone gets old.' Siddhartha had no idea. The palace was always filled with healthy young people.

The prince then saw a sick person. 'People suffer from sickness from time to time,' explained the servant. Siddhartha was alarmed. How did he not know about all this suffering?

Next, the pair came across a funeral procession. A dead person was wrapped in a sheet and was being carried by friends and relatives through the street. They were crying and wailing with grief. 'Everyone dies in the end,' explained the servant. Siddhartha became more and more depressed with all that he saw. He began to realise that suffering was an inevitable part of life and that everyone suffers, whoever they are.

Finally, the prince saw someone who gave him an idea which changed his future. Prince Siddhartha met a holy man. The man wore simple robes and was wandering the countryside. He had given up his home and his possessions, and he spent his time meditating and in calm concentration. The holy man was seeking to find out the truth about life and how to find peace. This meeting really made Siddhartha think about his own life.

When he returned to the palace he was very troubled about all that he had seen. How could he go on living his pampered existence in the palace when there was so much suffering in everyone's lives? And so he made a decision.

One night, when all were asleep, Prince Siddhartha left the palace and all his fine clothes and riches to live a simple, poor life and to seek the answer to life's suffering.

He gave up all worldly pleasures and ate and slept very little. He spent his time focusing his mind and meditating on life. He became very thin and weak, and realised that punishing his body and his health was not helping him to find the answers he was looking for. He realised that he needed to feed his body and to rest it. Siddhartha continued his life of meditation and concentration for many years.

One day, while he was sitting under a tree, in a deep meditative trance, Siddhartha had an amazing experience. After years and years of meditation his mind became crystal clear and he suddenly understood all about the nature of suffering and how people might overcome their suffering. He had become enlightened and he felt a wave of perfect bliss overcome him.

From this point on Siddhartha knew his mission in life was to share his enlightenment with others. He became a great teacher, travelling far and wide sharing his ideas and his wisdom. The people loved him and all that he taught them, and they called him the Buddha, the Enlightened Being.

Questions to prompt discussion

- Which part of the story do you think the *symbol* of the Buddha might represent?
- Do you think that is the most important part of the story? Why? Why not?
- How would you describe the facial expression on the image of the Buddha?
- Do you think that the expression is important to Buddhists? Why? Why not?
- What do you think the expression *symbolises* for Buddhists?

- Pupils can create drawings or clay models of images of the Buddha and produce labels to explain what the image *symbolises.*
- Show the picture of Buddhists in a shrine room (see CD artwork 7) and draw their ◀ attention to the activities of making offerings in front of the Buddha *rupa* (statue) as a sign of respect. Buddhists meditate, as the Buddha taught, in the shrine room.

Step 3 Evaluate

What is the value of the *symbol* of the Buddha to Buddhists and what issues are raised?

- Teachers should duplicate and cut up the cards and provide a set for each pair of pupils to sort. Pupils in pairs should look at the statements provided as CD Figure 5.5, ◀ decide which statements a Buddhist might agree with most, and sort them into an order of priority. There are no right or wrong answers here. Pupils should be encouraged to decide for themselves and be able to justify their ideas. Collate ideas in class discussion

Teachers duplicate and cut up the cards and provide a set for each pair of pupils to sort. Which statements might a Buddhist most strongly agree with? Put in order of priority.
The symbol of the Buddha helps Buddhists to feel peaceful
The symbol of the Buddha reminds Buddhists of the story about all the years he meditated.
The symbol of the Buddha makes the shrine room look attractive
The Buddha rupa (statue) helps everyone to focus attention on what is important.
The Buddha has a peaceful expression because it was easier for the artist to produce.
The Buddha rupa (statue) is a symbol of the goal of enlightenment.
The Buddha rupa (statue) symbolises that people can find release from suffering.
The Buddha rupa (statue) shows what the Buddha really looked like.
The Buddha rupa (statue) is so familiar that it has lost its symbolic meaning
The symbol of the Buddha is used by Buddhists all over the world.

Figure 5.5

Questions to prompt discussion

- Which do you think might be the most important statement for a Buddhist?
- Why do you think that?
- Are there any statements you could discard because they are not appropriate?
- Which are they?
- Why are they not appropriate?
- Do you think there might be other reasons why Buddhists value the *symbol* of the Buddha? What are they?
- Do you think there are any similarities between the symbols you created for Narnia and the Buddha *symbol*?
- What are the similarities?
- What are the differences?
- What other *symbol* could be used to remind Buddhists of the enlightenment of the Buddha?

Now go to Steps 4 and 5 in the book to complete the cycle of learning.

The symbol of water for Hindus

Pupils should explore Step 1 in the book (page 59) before they engage with Steps 2 and 3 in this section. This should then be followed by Steps 4 and 5 in the book (pages 63–64).

Step 2 Contextualise

How is the *symbol* of water used by Hindus?

- Show the class a picture of Hindus performing ritual washing in the River Ganges (see CD artwork 3). Pupils describe what they notice in the picture and speculate about the activities taking place.
- Pupils in pairs then discuss and speculate about why the water of the River Ganges is *symbolic* to Hindus.

Questions to prompt discussion

- What do you think the *symbol* of water in the Ganges might be used for?
- What do you think it might *symbolise* or mean to people?
- Why do you think that?
- Out of all the ideas that the class has suggested, do you think there are some ideas that are more likely than others? Why?

Tell the story (below and on CD) of the Holy River Ganges.

The Holy River Ganges

Many years ago lived a wise and benevolent king called Sagura who had 60,000 brave and honest sons. One day, the sons were out looking for their father's horse when they were all, except for one son, burned by the glare of an angry fortune teller who they had disturbed. They were instantly turned to ashes. This was a terrible way for them to die, and their souls would never find freedom.

In time King Sagura gave up his throne and his grandson became king. He had heard the terrible story of the 60,000 sons whose souls were trapped, and he was filled with sorrow. What could he do? The young king prayed to the powerful God, Lord Vishnu, for help.

Lord Vishnu took pity on the young king and ordered the River Goddess Ganga to go to earth. If the River from heaven, the Goddess Ganga, would go to earth, the souls of the 60,000 sons would be washed clean and pure and become free. But Ganga did not want to move. Lord Vishnu tried to persuade her; again and again he coaxed and encouraged her until she became very angry. She became so angry that eventually she plunged with thundering, churning waters towards the earth in a huge rage. If she crashed onto the earth with such ferocity the earth would be shattered and all would be lost.

Another God was looking on. The great God Shiva could see the earth in peril and moved swiftly. He caught the holy river Ganga in his long, black hair as she plunged towards the earth, and she became lost and tied up in the tangles and knots. When Ganga was finally released she was a calm river that flowed gently to the earth. The river flowed across India and found its way to the souls of the 60,000 sons. Their ashes were washed clean by the holy river and their souls were released to find eternal bliss. This holy river was the River Ganges.

Questions to prompt discussion

- Which part of the story do you think might be the most significant part for Hindus? Why?
- What do you think Hindus believe the water from the Ganges *symbolises*?
- How do you think Hindus might treat the water of the River Ganges? Why?

- The pupils should read the postcard from India (see CD and below fig 5.6) and discuss the information it contains.

Dear Sam,

Yesterday I went to a town on the River Ganges. It was amazing! The Ganges is a huge river and there were steps down to the water all along the river bank. There were loads of Hindu people there and some tourists, like us, taking pictures. Will send you a pic on your mobile.

The Hindu people were praying by the water and in the water. Some were washing in the water and others were sprinkling water over their heads and over their children. Some were filling bottles with Ganges water. Our guide said that they were taking it back to their relatives. When they wash in the river they believe that the things that they have done wrong in life will be washed away.

We even saw a funeral. A body was wrapped up in sheets and put on a pile of wood on the banks of the Ganges. There were loads of relatives and lots of flowers being sprinkled about and then the wood was set on fire. Our guide told us that the Ganges is very holy and when the ashes of a dead person are sprinkled on the river Ganges, their souls will be washed clean and be free for ever.

See you soon., Christa

Figure 5.6

- Pupils produce a display for the wall showing the Hindus performing their water rituals on the banks of the River Ganges. They should complete speech or thought bubbles for the Hindus illustrated on the display saying what the Ganges water *symbolises* for them.

Step 3 Evaluate

What is the value of the *symbol* of the water of the Ganges and what issues are raised?

- Duplicate and cut up the statements shown as Figure 5.6B on CD, to provide sets for pupils to sort. Working in pairs, pupils decide which statements a Hindu might agree with most, and sort them into an order of priority. There are no right or wrong answers here. Pupils should be encouraged to decide for themselves and be able to justify their ideas. Collate responses in class discussion.

Teachers duplicate and cut up the cards and provide a set for each pair of pupils to sort. Which statements might a Hindu most strongly agree with? Put in order of priority.
The symbol of water helps Hindus to feel peaceful
The symbol of the water of the Ganges reminds Hindus of the story about the power of the Goddess to wash souls clean.
The River Ganges is a beautiful river which gives life to the land.
The water of the Ganges symbolises purity and cleanliness
The water of the Ganges symbolically washes away any bad things I may have done in my life.
The water of the Ganges is a symbol of the Goddess Ganga
Hindus enjoy swimming in the River Ganges.
The symbol of water is so familiar that it has lost its symbolic meaning
The symbol of the water is used by Hindus all over the world.

Figure 5.6B

Questions to prompt discussion

- Which do you think might be the most important statement for a Hindu?
- Why do you think that?
- Are there any statements that you could discard because they are not appropriate?
- Which are they?
- Why are they not appropriate?
- Do you think there might be other reasons why Hindus value the *symbol* of water? What are they?
- Do you think there are any similarities between the *symbols* you created for Narnia and the *symbol* of the water of the Ganges?
- What are the similarities?
- What are the differences?
- What other *symbol* could be used to remind Hindus of the holy water of the river?

Now go to Steps 4 and 5 in the book to complete the cycle of learning.

The *symbol* of Ihram for Muslims

Pupils should explore Step 1 in the book (page 59) before they engage with Steps 2 and 3 in this section. This should then be followed by Steps 4 and 5 in the book (pages 63–64).

Step 2 Contextualise

How is the symbol of Ihram used by Muslims?

▶ ● Show the picture on CD (artwork 4) of a Muslim wearing the white robes of Ihram while they are on the Hajj (the pilgrimage to Makkah). Pupils describe what they notice in the picture, and speculate about the activities taking place and the reasons why the pilgrims might be wearing white robes.

● Pupils in pairs should discuss and speculate about what the white robes might *symbolise* to Muslims.

> **Questions to prompt discussion**
>
> ● What do you think the *symbol* of white robes might be used for?
> ● What do you think it might *symbolise* or mean to people?
> ● Why do you think that?
> ● Out of all the ideas that the class has suggested, do you think there are some ideas that are more likely than others? Why?

▶ ● Tell the story (below and on CD) of Anas going on the pilgrimage to Makkah.

Anas goes on pilgrimage

Anas was 18 years old. His parents had worked very hard and saved enough money for him to go, with his grandfather, on the great pilgrimage to Makkah. This is the journey of a lifetime for Muslims and a duty that all Muslims should carry out if they are able. It is called the Hajj.

Anas packed his bags ready for the journey. He would not need much, but the most important items were the two white pieces of cloth that are worn during the pilgrimage.

The journey went well; the flights were only delayed by half an hour and within a few hours Anas and his grandfather were checking into their hotel in Makkah. There was a feeling of great excitement in the hotel. All the hotel guests were Muslims. They had travelled from all over the world but they were all there together to share this wonderful experience. This was a time to feel close to Allah with fellow Muslims and to tread the same ground as the great prophet Muhammad had done in the holy city of Makkah.

The following morning Anas and his grandfather prepared themselves for the Hajj. To do so they had to feel thoroughly clean and pure. They bathed thoroughly, they had their hair trimmed and their nails cut at the barber's shop in the hotel. Anas had a shave but his grandfather just had his beard trimmed. They read passages from the Qu'ran, the holy book for Muslims, and they said prayers together. They were now in the sacred state of Ihram and they were ready to put on the special white clothes. These are two sheets of fabric with no stitching on them. One sheet is placed around the waist and held in place with a belt. The other is placed over the left shoulder and tied on the right hand side.

They were now both dressed in Ihram and in the holy state of Ihram, and ready to go on the Hajj together. During this time they would not cut their nails or their hair, they would not wear any perfume (aftershave or deodorant), they would not swear or get involved in any arguments, and they would concentrate on thinking about Allah. That was why they had come.

The pilgrimage was hard work. It was very hot, there were millions of people jostling and pushing and there was a lot of walking, day after day. But it was such a powerful experience for them both. They were thrilled to be with all these other Muslims, to be able to pray together, to visit the sites that Muhammad and other prophets had visited. They felt renewed in their beliefs and uplifted in their spirits.

As they travelled on their journey they could see that everyone was dressed the same. All the Muslims were wearing Ihram. The men wore two pieces of cloth, most of the women wore long white robes and had their heads covered. Anas could not tell who was rich and who was poor. He could not tell if he was standing next to a prince or a beggar, but it didn't matter. All people are equal in the eyes of Allah.

Questions to prompt discussion

- Which part of the story do you think makes reference to anything to do with the white robes?
- What do you think Muslims believe the white robes worn during Hajj *symbolise*?
- How do you think Muslims might treat the robes? Why?

- Pupils in pairs should take on the roles of a Muslim and a non-Muslim who are friends. The Muslim has just returned from the Hajj and is showing his or her friend pictures of themself dressed in white robes. The non-Muslim says, 'What are you wearing that crazy gear for?' How would the Muslim answer? Then the pupils should change roles.
- Pupils should complete a speech bubble to go with the picture (see CD for artwork Fig. 5.7) that explains the symbolism of wearing Ihram.

Step 3 Evaluate

What is the value of the *symbol* of the white robes and what issues are raised?

- Duplicate and cut up the statements shown as Figure 5.7B on CD, to provide sets for pupils to sort. Working in pairs, pupils decide which statements a Muslim might agree with most, and sort them into an order of priority. There are no right or wrong answers here. Pupils should be encouraged to decide for themselves and be able to justify their ideas. Collate responses in class discussion.

Teachers duplicate and cut up the cards and provide a set for each pair of pupils to sort. Which statements might a Muslim most strongly agree with? Put in order of priority.

The symbolic white robes help Muslims to feel the same as everyone else.
The symbolic white robes remind Muslims that they are all equal in the eyes of Allah.
The white robes make everyone look clean and neat.
The white robes symbolise purity and a state of holiness.
The white robes are a symbol to remind Muslims that Allah can provide for them.
The white robes are a symbol to remind them that they should share things with other Muslims.
Muslims enjoy wearing the white robes.
The symbolic white robes are so familiar that that they have lost their symbolic meaning.
The symbolic white robes are used by Muslims from all over the world.
The white robes are only worn by Muslims who have been on the Hajj, the pilgrimage to Makkah.

Figure 5.7B

Questions to prompt discussion

- Which do you think might be the most important statement for a Muslim?
- Why do you think that?
- Are there any statements that you could discard because they are not appropriate?
- Which are they?
- Why are they not appropriate?
- Do you think there might be other reasons why Muslims value the *symbol* of white robes? What are they?
- Do you think there are any similarities between the *symbols* you created for Narnia and the *symbol* of the white robes?
- What other *symbols* could be used to remind Muslims of their state of purity and equality with others when they are on the Hajj?

Now go to Steps 4 and 5 in the book to complete the cycle of learning.

The symbol of bread for Jews

Pupils should explore Step 1 in the book (page 59) before they engage with Steps 2 and 3 in this section. This should then be followed by Steps 4 and 5 in the book (pages 63–64).

Step 2 Contextualise

How is the *symbol* of bread used by Jews?

- Show the picture (see CD artwork 5) of a Jewish family sharing the two loaves of ◀ bread (Challot) at the Friday evening meal at the start of Shabbat (the Sabbath). Pupils describe what they notice in the picture and speculate about the activities taking place.
- Pupils in pairs discuss and speculate about why the bread might be *symbolic* to Jews.

Questions to prompt discussion

- What do you think the *symbol* of bread might be used for?
- What do you think it might *symbolise* or mean to people?
- Why do you think that?
- Out of all the ideas that the class has suggested, do you think there are some ideas that are more likely than others? Why?

- Tell the Jewish story of the Creation (see below and CD).   ◀

The story of Creation

In the beginning there was nothing but darkness. The darkness was empty.

On the first day God created light so that there was darkness and light. God called the light 'day' and the dark he called 'night'.

On the second day God created the sky and put it over the Earth.

On the third day God created dry land and sea. God created plants and trees to grow on the earth.

On the fourth day God made the sun, the moon and the stars to shine in the sky.

On the fifth day God made all the creatures to swim in the seas and all the birds to fly in the sky.

On the sixth day God created all the animals that live on the earth and he made a man and a woman. God told the man and the woman that they were in charge of the fish, the birds and all the wild animals, and that the grains and the fruits from the plants and trees were for food.

By the seventh day God had finished his work and he set the seventh day apart from the others and made it a special holy day.

Questions to prompt discussion

- Which part of the story do you think makes reference to anything to do with bread?
- What do you think Jews believe the bread on their table at Shabbat *symbolises*?
- How do you think Jews might treat the bread? Why?

- Role play or demonstrate a Jewish Friday night meal with the class, or show a clip from a DVD or a website. Draw attention to the father removing the special cloth over the two loaves and saying a blessing: '*Blessed are You, Adonai our God, Ruler of the world, who brings forth bread from the earth.*' The father then cuts or tears the bread and distributes it to members of the family and they all eat it together, thinking about the blessing.
- ▶ The pupils should complete a thought or speech bubble (see CD artwork Fig 5.8) for members of the family to put on the picture to complete the phrase, 'For me, the bread *symbolises* …'

Step 3 Evaluate

What is the value of the symbol of the bread and what issues are raised?

- ▶ Duplicate and cut up the statements shown as Figure 5.9 on the CD, to provide sets for pupils to sort. Working in pairs, pupils decide which statements a Jew might agree with most, and sort them into an order of priority. There are no right or wrong answers here. Pupils should be encouraged to decide for themselves and be able to justify their ideas. Collate responses in class discussion.

Teachers duplicate and cut up the cards and provide a set for each pair of pupils to sort. Which statements might a Jew most strongly agree with? Put in order of priority.
The symbol of bread helps Jews to feel full up.
The symbol of the bread reminds Jews of the story about the power of God creating the world and everything in it.
The bread provides a lovely smell during the Shabbat meal.
The bread symbolises purity
The bread is a symbol to remind Jews that God can provide for them.
The bread is a symbol to remind them that they should share things in the family
Jews enjoy the taste of the bread.
The symbol of bread is so familiar that it has lost its symbolic meaning
The symbol of the bread is used by Jews all over the world.
The bread is a symbol used to help Jews to remember to keep God's commandments.

Figure 5.9

Questions to prompt discussion

- Which do you think might be the most important statement for a Jew?
- Why do you think that?
- Are there any statements that you could discard because they are not appropriate?
- Which are they?
- Why are they not appropriate?
- Do you think there might be other reasons why Jews value the *symbol* of bread? What are they?
- Do you think there are any similarities between the *symbols* you created for Narnia and the *symbol* of the bread?
- What are the similarities?
- What are the differences?
- What other *symbol* could be used to remind Jews of God's creation?

Now go to Steps 4 and 5 in the book (pages 63–64) to complete the cycle of learning.

The symbol of the Kirpan for Sikhs

Pupils should explore Step 1, in the book (page 59) before they engage with Steps 2 and 3 in this section. This should then be followed by Steps 4 and 5 in the booklet (pages 63–64).

Step 2 Contextualise

How is the symbol of the Kirpan used by Sikhs?
- Show the picture on CD (artwork 6) of a Sikh wearing a Kirpan (a symbolic sword). ◀
  Pupils should describe what they notice in the picture and speculate about the possible reasons for wearing a Kirpan.
- Pupils in pairs discuss and speculate about why the Kirpan might be *symbolic* to Sikhs.

Questions to prompt discussion

- What do you think the *symbol* of the kirpan might be used for?
- What do you think it might *symbolise* or mean to people?
- Why do you think that?
- Out of all the ideas that the class has suggested, do you think there are some ideas that are more likely than others? Why?

 ● Tell the Sikh story of Guru Gobind Singh (see below and CD).

Guru Gobind Singh and the Khalsa

Every year all the Sikh people met together to hear their great leader. So here they all were in a vast field and at the front was a large tent opening onto a platform. People jostled and joked with each other. They were looking forward to hearing their leader, Guru Gobind Singh, speak to them and share his wisdom.

At last out stepped the great man and the crowd gave a gasp. He was waving a large sword above his head.

'I want a brave Sikh to step forward. Who is willing to give up his life for God and for his faith?' The crowd fell still and silent. Again the leader called, 'I want a brave Sikh to step forward. Who would be willing to give up his life for his God?' There was a slight movement among the people, and slowly a man walked up to Guru Gobind Singh. Into the tent they went and the crowd heard a terrifying swish of the sword and a thud. The crowd held its breath.

Out of the tent swept Guru Gobind Singh, once more. Again he was waving his sword, which was now dripping with blood. Again he made his terrifying demand and again a brave man stepped out of the crowd and followed their great leader into the tent. 'What is happening?' the people murmured. 'Has our leader gone mad?'

Five times it happened, and five brave men stepped forward and went into the tent with Guru Gobind Singh. Each time the crowd heard the sound of the swishing sword. They were really alarmed and some began to turn to leave. Was the Guru going to kill all his people? But then something amazing happened. Out of the tent walked the five brave men. They were all dressed alike and all wearing turbans on their heads. The Guru pulled back the tent flap and inside were five beheaded goats. 'Today we will start a new brotherhood and call it the Khalsa,' explained Guru Gobind Singh. 'I want Sikhs to be brave like these five brave men who are the Beloved Five. To show that we are Sikhs we will not cut our hair. We will keep our hair tidy with a special comb and we will wear turbans over our hair. We will wear a steel bangle and wear a sword to show that we are brave and that we will protect the weak and defend our freedom.

A special ceremony then took place. A bowl was filled with sweetened water which was stirred with the sword. Men drank from the blessed water and as they did so, they became new members of the Khalsa, the special brotherhood of Sikhism.

Questions to prompt discussion

- Which part of the story do you think might be the most significant part for Sikhs? Why?
- What do you think Sikhs believe the sword (Kirpan) *symbolises*?
- How do you think Sikhs might use the *symbolic* sword (Kirpan)? Why?

- The pupils should investigate websites and books for images and information about the Kirpan and when it is used.
- If possible, the teacher should invite a Sikh into class to talk to the pupils about the Kirpan, why it is worn and what it *symbolises* for them.

- The teacher should ask the pupils to imagine that they are a Sikh boy or girl and that the police have stopped them and found that they are wearing a Kirpan. The police want to confiscate it. What does the Sikh say about this? Pupils should role play the conversation between the police and the Sikh.

Step 3 Evaluate

What is the value of the *symbol* of the Kirpan and what issues are raised?

- Duplicate and cut up the statements shown as Figure 5.10 on CD, to provide sets for ◀ pupils to sort. Working in pairs, pupils decide which statements a Sikh might agree with most, and sort them into an order of priority. There are no right or wrong answers here. Pupils should be encouraged to decide for themselves and be able to justify their ideas. Collate responses in class discussion.

Teachers duplicate and cut up the cards and provide a set for each pair of pupils to sort. Which statements might a Sikh most strongly agree with? Put in order of priority.
The symbol of Kirpan helps Sikhs to feel brave.
The symbol of the Kirpan reminds Sikhs of the story about Guru Gobind Singh and the Khalsa.
The Kirpan is very dangerous
The Kirpan symbolises purity
The Kirpan is a symbol to remind Sikhs that they are united.
The Kirpan is a symbol to remind them that they should defend their faith and their freedom.
Sikhs enjoy wearing the Kirpan.
The symbol of Kirpan is so familiar that it has lost its symbolic meaning
The symbol of the Kirpan is used by Sikhs all over the world.
The Kirpan is a symbol used to help Sikhs to remember people who are poor or weak.

Figure 5.10

Questions to prompt discussion

- Which do you think might be the most important statement for a Sikh?
- Why do you think that?
- Are there any statements that you could discard because they are not appropriate?
- Which are they?
- Why are they not appropriate?
- Do you think there might be other reasons why Sikhs value the *symbol* of the Kirpan? What are they?
- Do you think there are any similarities between the *symbols* you created for Narnia and the *symbol* of the kirpan?
- What are the similarities?
- What are the differences?
- What other *symbol* could be used to remind Sikhs to defend their faith and people who may be weak?

Now go to Steps 4 and 5 in the book (pages 63–64) to complete the cycle of learning.

Resources on the CD

Figures

5.2   Writing frame – *A symbol is something that ...*
5.3   Cards – What is the value of the symbol of the empty cross?
5.4   Writing frame – *This symbol is important to me*
5.5   Cards – What is the value of the symbol of the Buddha?
5.6   Postcard from India
5.6B Cards – What is the value of the symbol of the water of the Ganges?
5.7   Speech bubble to be placed on artwork 4
5.7B Cards – What is the value of the symbol of the white robes?
5.8   Speech bubble to be placed on artwork 5
5.9   Cards – What is the value of the symbol of the bread?
5.10 Cards – What is the value of the symbol of the Kirpan

Artwork

1a.   Crucifix
1b.   Plain cross
2.   The Buddha
3.   Ritual washing in the River Ganges
4.   The white robes of Ihram
5.   Jewish family sharing the two loaves of bread
6.   A Sikh wearing a Kirpan
7.   Buddhists in a shrine room

Stories: Christian

The Easter story
The story of Creation

Stories: Buddhist

The life of the Buddha

Stories: Hindu

The Holy River Ganges

Stories: Muslim

Anas goes on pilgrimage

Stories: Sikh

Guru Gobind Singh and the Khalsa

Concept: *ritual*

This concept resonates with many pupils for they can often identify *rituals* in their own lives and appreciate their importance. The key to their enquiry into this concept is to help them to recognise that *rituals* are not the same as routines, but that they are symbolic acts and have particular significance which may not always be obvious to an outsider. The unit enables pupils to investigate what *rituals* are and why they are meaningful to individuals and groups of people, both religious and non-religious. In the book the example of the sharing of bread and wine during the Eucharist/Communion service is explored as a potent *ritual* for Christians. This is followed by examples of how *ritual* can be explored within aspects of other major religions.

The *ritual* of puja for Buddhists
The *ritual* of arti for Hindus
The *ritual* of salah for Muslims
The *ritual* of using tefillin for Jews
The *rituals* of amrit for Sikhs

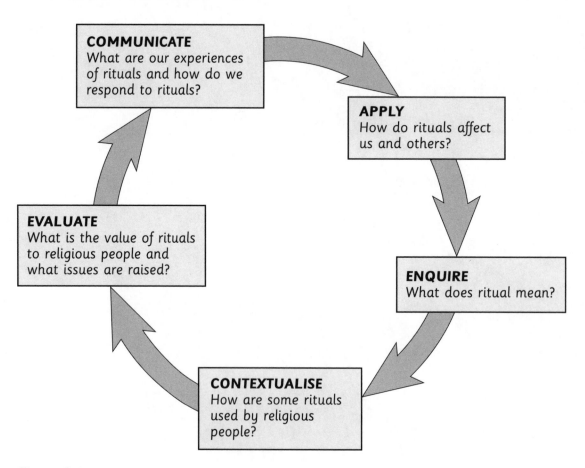

Figure 6.1

The ritual of the Eucharist for Christians

Step 1 Enquire

What does *ritual* mean?

- Pupils in groups brainstorm the word *ritual* on large sheets of paper. On the reverse of the paper they should brainstorm the word 'routine'. Are they the same? Are there any differences? Pupils may be guided through discussion or a 'community of enquiry' to help them to develop their interpretation of the concept.
- Duplicate and prepare sets of the cards shown as Figure 6.2 and on CD. Pupils in ◀ groups each have a set of cards to discuss and sort into what they think are routines and what they think are *rituals*. Compare the groups' lists in class discussion.

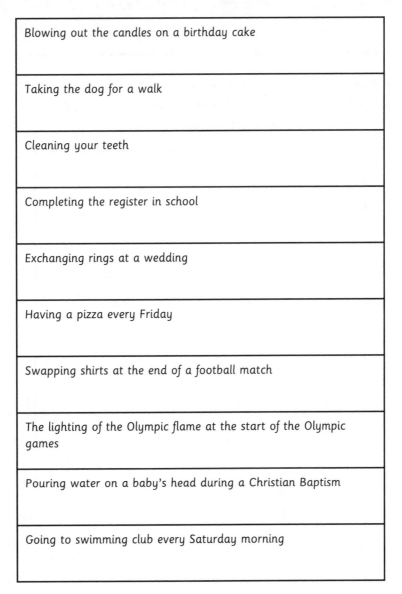

| Blowing out the candles on a birthday cake |
| Taking the dog for a walk |
| Cleaning your teeth |
| Completing the register in school |
| Exchanging rings at a wedding |
| Having a pizza every Friday |
| Swapping shirts at the end of a football match |
| The lighting of the Olympic flame at the start of the Olympic games |
| Pouring water on a baby's head during a Christian Baptism |
| Going to swimming club every Saturday morning |

Figure 6.2

Questions to prompt discussion when pupils are discussing and sorting their cards

- Does the activity on the card happen regularly? Why? Why not? Does that make it a routine or a *ritual*?
- Does the activity on the card have any practical purpose? (For instance, do footballers change their shirts because they want a clean one? Do people light the candles on the birthday cake because there is a power cut? Do vicars pour water over the baby's head at a Christening because the baby has dirty hair?) Does that make it a routine or a *ritual*?
- Does the activity have any particular meaning that is not obvious?
- What does the activity mean to the people who are doing it? Does that make it a routine or a *ritual*?

- Pupils write definitions or descriptions in groups for the concept *ritual* (see the writing frame shown as Figure 6.3 and on CD) and as a class decide on a class definition for *ritual*. Display this in the classroom for future reference.

A ritual is something that.......

Figure 6.3

Step 2 Contextualise

How do Christians perform the *ritual* of the Eucharist, or Communion?

- Show the pupils a chalice and paten (see CD artwork 1). and ask them to speculate about what these objects are, who might use them, where they might be used, what they might be used for, and when and why. The class should discuss their ideas without the teacher offering any answers at this point.
- Tell the story of the Last Supper (below and on the CD) to pupils.

The Last Supper

Jesus was with his twelve followers in a room which had been prepared for them. They were going to celebrate the Passover meal together. During the meal Jesus took a piece of bread and said a prayer of thanks. Then he broke the bread and gave it to all his followers. 'Take this and eat it. It is my body,' he said. 'Do this in memory of me.' Jesus's followers ate the bread.

Then Jesus took a cup of wine, said a prayer of thanks and passed it to his followers. 'Take this and drink it, all of you. It is my blood which is poured out for many people for the forgiveness of their sins.' Jesus's followers all drank wine from the cup. Jesus then said, 'I will not drink wine again until I drink new wine with you in my father's kingdom.'

Later on, after the meal, Jesus went with his friends into the garden of Gethsemane where he was arrested. He was later put on trial and sentenced to death by hanging on a cross.

Three days later, when some women went to visit Jesus's tomb his body was not there. An angel told them that Jesus had come alive again after he had died. Later on some of Jesus's followers saw Jesus and spoke with him.

Questions to prompt discussion

- Can you see any link between this story and the chalice and paten that we looked at?
- What sort of *ritual* might some Christians use these items for, do you think?
- Why do you think that some Christians might carry out this *ritual*?

- Pupils research the ritual of the sharing of bread and wine during the Eucharist or Communion using websites or books, or invite a Christian to explain the *ritual*. Alternatively, invite a vicar or a priest to demonstrate the *ritual* for pupils.
- Pupils should produce simple instructions for a Christian child who is about to participate in their first Eucharist or Communion *ritual*. Pupils should make reference to the meaning of the *ritual* for Christians.

Step 3 **Evaluate**

What is the value of the *ritual* of sharing bread and wine to Christians, and what issues are raised?

- Pupils look at artists' impressions of the Last Supper selected by the teacher from a website or a book.

Questions to prompt discussion

- What do you notice about these pictures?
- Are they all exactly the same? Does that matter? Why? Why not?
- Why do you think there are a number of pictures of this event?
- Why do you think this event is important to Christians?
- Why do you think Christians re-enact the *ritual* of sharing bread and wine in churches today?
- How do you think Christians might feel if they could not participate in the *ritual*? Would it matter? Why? Why not?

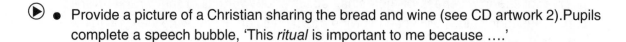

- Provide a picture of a Christian sharing the bread and wine (see CD artwork 2). Pupils complete a speech bubble, 'This *ritual* is important to me because ....'

Step 4 **Communicate**

What are our experiences of *rituals* and how do we respond to *rituals*?

- Pupils consider *rituals* in their own experience, such as lighting and blowing out birthday candles. They may want to draw on other *rituals* that they know about, such as the *ritual* bow after a judo match, changing shirts with the opposing team after a football match, or exchanging rings.

Questions to prompt discussion

- Are these *rituals* or routines? (Pupils should refer to the definition in Step 1.)
- How does each *ritual* make the participants feel, and what is the meaning behind *it*?

- As a class or in groups, pupils should think of a significant event (such as the first day of summer, or the crowning of a new king) and plan a *ritual* that might be carried out every year to mark the event.
- Pupils role play their ideas. Other members of the class speculate about the event that is being marked. Can they identify the meaning of the event, or is that only evident to the participants?
- The class should discuss: if the event turned out not to be positive (for instance, if the summer was cold and wet, or a cruel king was crowned) would people still want to mark the event with a *ritual*? Why? Why not?

Step 5 **Apply**

How do *rituals* affect us and others?

● Have a class debate about *rituals.* Pupils should prepare for the debate by discussing in pairs their ideas in favour of and against the motion on the format provided (see CD and Figure 6.4).

The motion is:
Rituals are time wasting and should be banned

Figure 6.4

The *ritual* of puja for Buddhists

Pupils should explore Step 1 in the book (pages 83–84) before they engage with Steps 2 and 3 in this section. This should then be followed by Steps 4 and 5 in the book (pages 86–87).

Step 2 **Contextualise**

How do Buddhists perform the *ritual* of puja?

● Show the pupils the items that are found in a Buddhist temple (Mahayana tradition) which are used for *ritual* worship, devotion or reflection (see artwork 3 on CD).

- The pupils should speculate in pairs how they think the items might be used in a *ritual* and what the *ritual* helps Buddhists to focus on.
- Compare ideas in class discussion.

Questions to prompt discussion

- What do you think these objects might be used for?
- Where might you find them?
- What do you think they might mean to people when they are used in a *ritual*?
- Why do you think that?
- Out of all the ideas that the class has suggested, do you think there are some ideas that are more likely than others? Why?

- Distribute or show on an interactive whiteboard the information below about the seven parts of the *ritual* of puja (worship or devotion) from the Mahayana tradition of Buddhism (see CD).

Buddhist puja

1 A Buddhist bows down in front of images and statues of the Buddha and other revered beings (bodhisattvas) to honour them.
2 Offerings are made at the shrine. There are frequently seven bowls of water which represent seven offerings:
   - water for drinking
   - water for washing the feet
   - perfumed water for a bath
   - sweet-smelling incense
   - flowers
   - light
   - food (this is sometimes real food such as fruit or rice, and is not represented by water).

   Music might be another offering, and is represented by the ringing of a bell or small cymbals. All these items are ones that would be provided for an honoured guest to someone's home.
3 A Buddhist then considers and confesses to anything they have done or thought that was unhelpful, and seeks help from the Buddha or the other revered beings (bodhisattvas) to enable them to achieve better actions and thoughts in the future.
4 A Buddhist reflects on the sense of wellbeing and joy which comes with knowing about the goodness of the Buddha and being reminded of his example.
5 A Buddhist then asks the Buddha and the other revered beings (bodhisattvas) for guidance in the way to live.
6 A Buddhist worshipper then asks the Buddha and the bodhisattvas to stay active in the world and continue to guide all beings.
7 If Buddhists have earned any praise or merit for their worship or devotion, they ask that it be shared for the goodness of all beings. This is a reminder that their worship should never be the cause of selfishness or pride.

Questions to prompt discussion

- Did any of you make good guesses about the uses of the items in the Buddhist *rituals*?
- Which part of the *ritual* do you think might be most important to a Buddhist? Why?
- How would you describe the feelings of the Buddhist participating in this *ritual*?

- The pupils could create a diagram or drawing of the shrine in a Buddhist temple (Mahayana tradition), and label the items describing how they are used in the *ritual* of puja. Alternatively, the teacher could produce a large wall display of an empty shrine and pupils contribute drawings of the different items. The pupils could produce labels of explanations using ICT about how the items are used in the *ritual.*

Step 3 Evaluate

What is the value of the Buddhist *ritual* and what issues are raised?

- The teacher should outline the following scenario to the pupils for discussion:

Imagine that the Buddhist monks go early in the morning to open up the shrine room to prepare it for the worshippers who will arrive later. When they enter the shrine room they are astounded. All the items that are used for ritual worship have been removed. They have been robbed during the night. The large statues have gone, the bowls have gone, the flowers are scattered on the floor. The worshippers from the village will be arriving soon. What will they do?

- The pupils in pairs or threes should discuss what the monks should do.
- Collate their ideas in a class discussion.

Questions to prompt discussion

- Would the monks and the other worshippers still be able to perform their *rituals*?
- Would they feel the same about their *rituals* without the statues and the other items?
- Why? Why not?
- Which do you think might be the most important part of the *ritual* for a Buddhist?
- Why do you think that?
- Are there any parts of the *rituals* that you think could be left out? Which are they? Why have you thought of those particular parts?
- How do you think Buddhists might feel if they were unable to participate in their *rituals*?
- What difference might it make to them?

- Duplicate and distribute the image provided (see CD artwork 4), Pupils should complete the speech bubble for the Buddhist, 'The *rituals* of puja are important to me because ....'

Now go to Steps 4 and 5 in the book to complete the cycle of learning.

The *ritual* of *arti* for Hindus

Pupils should explore Step 1 in the book (pages 83–84) before they engage with Steps 2 and 3 in this section. This should then be followed by Steps 4 and 5 in the book (pages 86–87).

Step 2 Contextualise

How do Hindus perform the ritual of arti?

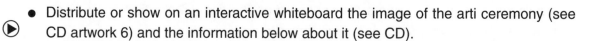

- Show the pupils an arti lamp (See CD artwork 5).
- Pupils should speculate in pairs how they think it might be used in a *ritual* and what the *ritual* helps Hindus to focus on.
- Compare their ideas in class discussion.

> **Questions to prompt discussion**
>
> - What do you think this object might be used for?
> - Where might you find it?
> - What do you think it might mean to people when it is used in a *ritual*?
> - Why do you think that?
> - Out of all the ideas that the class has suggested, do you think there are some ideas that are more likely than others? Why?

- Distribute or show on an interactive whiteboard the image of the arti ceremony (see CD artwork 6) and the information below about it (see CD).

> ### *The arti ceremony*
>
> 1 The Hindu priest lights the wicks in the five sections of the arti lamp. Some Hindus say that the flames represent earth, air, fire, water and ether. The flames are purifying.
> 2 Hindu worshippers are seated on the floor facing the shrines which contain the images of the Hindu deities (representations of God).
> 3 The priest takes the lamp and waves it in a steady, circular motion in front of the statues of each of the deities in the temple shrines.
> 4 Prayers are said by the priest and worshippers as the priest performs the arti *ritual* with the lamp. The flames represent the prayers going up to God. Part of the prayer is:
>
> *Whoever meditates upon you receives your grace. The worries of his mind will disappear; his home will be blessed with peace, happiness and plenty and his bodily pains will go. Wipe out our sins, increase our devotion and faith. May we serve you and serve others who serve you.*
>
> 5 When the priest has performed the *ritual* in front of the deities he brings the arti lamp to the worshippers in the temple. Worshippers wave their hands gently over the flames, gathering God's blessings, and smooth their hands over their heads and faces in a gesture which represents them pouring God's blessings and glory over themselves.

Questions to prompt discussion

- Did any of you make good guesses about the uses of the arti lamp in the Hindu *rituals*?
- Which part of the *ritual* do you think might be most important to a Hindu? Why?
- How would you describe the feelings of the Hindu participating in this *ritual*?

- Pupils should draw a priest in front of one of the shrines in a Hindu temple and annotate their drawing, describing the *ritual* of the arti ceremony.

Step 3 Evaluate

What is the value of the Hindu *ritual* and what issues are raised?

- The teacher should outline the following scenario to the pupils for discussion:

Imagine that the Hindu priest goes early in the morning to open up the shrine room to prepare it for the worshippers who will arrive later. However, the arti lamp is missing. He hunts high and low but it cannot be found. What will he do about the arti ritual?

- Pupils in pairs or threes should discuss what the priest might do.
- Collate their ideas in class discussion.

Questions to prompt discussion

- Would the arti *ritual* still be able to take place?
- How?
- Would the priest and worshippers feel the same about their *rituals* without the arti lamp?
- Why? Why not?
- Which do you think might be the most important part of the *ritual* for a Hindu?
- Why do you think that?
- Are there any parts of the *ritual* that you think could be left out? Which are they? Why have you thought of those particular parts?
- How do you think Hindus might feel if they were unable to participate in their *rituals*?
- What difference might it make to them?

- Duplicate and distribute the image provided (see CD artwork 7). Pupils complete the speech bubble for the Hindu, 'The *rituals* of arti are important to me because ....'

Now go to Steps 4 and 5 in the book to complete the cycle of learning.

The *ritual* of salah for Muslims

Pupils should explore Step 1 in the book (pages 83–84) before they engage with Steps 2 and 3 in this section. This should then be followed by Steps 4 and 5 in the book (pages 86–87).

Step 2 Contextualise

How do Muslims perform the *ritual* of salah?

- Show pupils the picture (see CD artwork 8) of Muslims performing their *ritual* prayers together. Pupils in pairs discuss and speculate about what *ritual* the Muslims are performing and what it might mean to Muslims.

> ### Questions to prompt discussion
>
> - What do you think Muslims are doing this *ritual* for?
> - What do you think it might mean to them?
> - Why do you think that?
> - Out of all the ideas that the class has suggested, do you think there are some ideas that are more likely than others? Why?

- Distribute or show on an interactive whiteboard the information below about salah for pupils to explore (see CD).

> ### The Muslim ritual prayer, salah
>
> 1 Salah is one of the Five Pillars (duties) for all Muslims to follow. It reminds Muslims that they belong to Allah (God). Muslims pray in order to praise Allah and remind themselves that Allah should be uppermost in their thoughts.
> 2 Salah takes place, for Muslims all over the world, five times a day. The times are daybreak, noon, afternoon, the close of day and at night. The Qur'an (the Muslim holy book) says:
>
> *Glory be to Allah when you reach evening and when you arise in the morning. Praise belongs to him in heaven and on earth; glorify him in the late afternoon and when you enter the noon hour. (Qur'an 30:18)*
>
> 3 Muslims know when it is a prayer time because they hear the 'call to prayer' which can be heard from the mosque all over Muslim towns and cities.
> 4 Muslims prepare for prayer by washing thoroughly and focusing on Allah.
> 5 Muslims may perform salah alone or with others, or in large groups in the mosque. They face the holy city of Makkah when they perform the salah ritual.
> 6 All Muslims say the same prayers in the same prayer positions together. They stand with their hands facing forward each side of their faces, they kneel and they touch the ground in front of them with their foreheads, saying prayers in praise of Allah throughout. The full sequence of salah has twelve prayer positions. This sequence is called a rakat.

Questions to prompt discussion

- Did any of you make good guesses about the Muslim prayer *rituals*?
- Which part of the *ritual* do you think might be most important to a Muslim? Why?
- How would you describe the feelings of the Muslim participating in this *ritual*?

- The pupils should produce a very simple guide for a Muslim child about how to perform the salah *ritual*.

Step 3 Evaluate

What is the value of the Muslim prayer *ritual* and what issues are raised?

- Outline the following scenario to the pupils for discussion:

Imagine that a Muslim is unwell and has to take to his bed. He feels so ill that he is unable to stand. He will not be able to perform the prayer rituals. What will he do?

- The pupils in pairs or threes should discuss what the sick Muslim should do.

Questions to prompt discussion

- Would it matter if the Muslim was unable to perform the salah prayer *ritual*?
- Why? Why not?
- How do you think he would feel about not being able to do the *ritual*?
- What difference would it make to him?
- Which do you think might be the most important part of the *ritual* for a Muslim?
- Why do you think that?
- Are there any parts of the *ritual* that you think could be left out? Which are they? Why have you thought of those particular parts?

- Duplicate and distribute the image provided (see CD artwork 9). Pupils complete the speech bubble for the Muslim, 'The *rituals* of salah are important to me because ....'

Now go to Steps 4 and 5 in the book to complete the cycle of learning.

The *ritual* of using tefillin for Jews

Pupils should explore Step 1 in the book (pages 83–84) before they engage with Steps 2 and 3 in this section. This should then be followed by Steps 4 and 5 in the book (pages 86–87).

Step 2 Contextualise

How do Jews use the tefillin in a *ritual*?

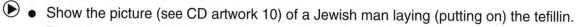

- Show the picture (see CD artwork 10) of a Jewish man laying (putting on) the tefillin.
- Pupils in pairs should discuss and speculate about why the *ritual* of putting on the tefillin might be important to Jews.

Questions to prompt discussion

- What do you think the *ritual* might be for?
- What do you think it might mean to Jews?
- Why do you think that?
- Out of all the ideas that the class has suggested, do you think there are some ideas that are more likely than others? Why?

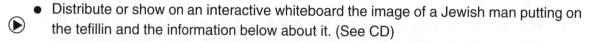

- Distribute or show on an interactive whiteboard the image of a Jewish man putting on the tefillin and the information below about it. (See CD)

The ritual of laying the tefillin

1   Each morning many Jewish men and older boys (and sometimes women and girls) put on their prayer shawls and skull caps and their tefillin. This is because they are keeping one of God's laws which says:

Hear O Israel, the Lord our God is one.
You shall love the Lord your God with all your heart, with all your soul and with all your might.
These words which I command you this day shall be in your heart …. You shall bind them for a sign upon your hand, and they shall be between your eyes. (Deuteronomy 6: 4–8)

2   The tefillin are two hard leather boxes which contain the words of a commandment from God called the Shema (see above for the Shema). The boxes have long leather straps. The straps of one box are wrapped around the left arm with the box at the top of the arm. The other box is strapped around the head so that the box rests on the forehead.

3   While the tefillin are being wrapped around the head and the arm, the Jew concentrates on God and offers prayers. Here is a shortened version of a prayer, which would be said in Hebrew.

By putting on the tefillin I intend to fulfil the command of my creator, who has commanded us to wear the tefillin, as it is written in the Torah …. He has commanded us to wear the tefillin on the arm in memory of his outstretched arm, opposite the heart to show that our hearts' desires should be to the service of God. The mind which is in the brain and all senses ought to be in God's service …

4   Prayers are offered three times a day: in the morning, at noon and in the evening.

Questions to prompt discussion

- Did any of you make good guesses about the use of the tefillin in a *ritual*?
- Which part of the *ritual* do you think might be most important to a Jew? Why?
- How would you describe the feelings of the Jew participating in this *ritual*?

- The pupils should produce a very simple guide for a Jewish child about how to perform the ritual of the laying of the tefillin.

Step 3 Evaluate

What is the value of the Jewish *ritual* of laying the tefillin and what issues are raised?

- Outline the following scenario to the pupils for discussion.

Imagine that a Jewish man has had his tefillin for many years. They are treasured items that were given to him by his grandfather. The tefillin are very old now and the leather is very frayed. As he starts to wrap the tefillin around his arm the leather strap breaks in a few places and the box falls to the floor. It falls apart as it hits the floor. It cannot possibly be used now. What will he do?

- The class should discuss this situation in pairs or threes.

Questions to prompt discussion

- Would it matter if the Jew was unable to perform the *ritual* of laying the tefillin? Why? Why not?
- How do you think he would feel about not being able to do the *ritual*?
- What difference would it make to him?
- Which do you think might be the most important part of the *ritual* for a Jew?
- Why do you think that?
- Are there any parts of the *ritual* that you think could be left out?
- Which are they? Why have you thought of those particular parts?

- Duplicate and distribute the image provided (see CD artwork 11). Pupils complete the ◀ speech bubble for the Jew, 'The *rituals* of tefillin are important to me because ….'

Now go to Steps 4 and 5 in the book (pages 86–87) to complete the cycle of learning.

The *ritual* of amrit for Sikhs

Pupils should explore Step 1 in the book (pages 83–84) before they engage with Steps 2 and 3 in this section. This should then be followed by Steps 4 and 5 in the book (pages 86–87).

Step 2 Contextualise

How do Sikhs perform the *ritual* of amrit?

● Show the picture (see CD artwork 12) of a Sikh performing an amrit *ritual* for a Sikh joining the Khalsa.
● The pupils in pairs should discuss and speculate about what *ritual* the Sikhs are performing and what it might mean to them.

> ### Questions to prompt discussion
>
> ● What do you think Sikhs are doing this *ritual* for?
> ● What do you think it might mean to them?
> ● Why do you think that?
> ● Out of all the ideas that the class has suggested, do you think there are some ideas that are more likely than others? Why?

● Distribute or show on an interactive whiteboard the image of Sikhs performing amrit *rituals* and the information below about it. (See CD)

> ### *The amrit ritual*
>
> 1 The amrit *ritual* takes place when a Sikh joins the Khalsa, which is the name for the Sikh fellowship. Not all Sikhs join the Khalsa.
> 2 Five Sikhs are present to represent the Panje Piare (the 'five beloved ones' who were the first five brave Sikhs who joined the very first Khalsa in 1699).
> 3 Passages from the Guru Granth Sahib (the Sikh holy book) are read.
> 4 One of the five men lists the duties of members of the Khalsa.
> 5 The Sikh who is joining the Khalsa kneels on his/her right knee, and all that are present drink *amrit* from a large bowl which is passed around. Amrit is the name of the sweetened water which is the central part of the *ritual*.
> 6 The sweetened water in the bowl (amrit) is then sprinkled over the head and hands of the new member and prayers are said.
> 7 All the Sikhs present share a little kara prashad, which is a sweet mixture made from semolina or flour. Eating together demonstrates that all Sikhs are equal, and the sweetness of the food is a reminder that it is God's wish to bless humankind.

> **Questions to prompt discussion**
>
> - Did any of you make good guesses about the Sikh *ritual*?
> - Which part of the *ritual* do you think might be most important to a Sikh? Why?
> - How would you describe the feelings of the Sikh participating in this *ritual*?

- Duplicate and distribute to the pupils the picture of a Sikh participating in the amrit *ritual* (see CD artwork 12). Pupils create labels describing the different features of the *ritual*.

Step 3 Evaluate

What is the value of the amrit *ritual* to Sikhs, and what issues are raised?

- Outline the following scenario to the pupils for discussion.

Imagine that a Sikh is all prepared to take part in the amrit ritual to become a member of the Khalsa. He is ready to take on new responsibilities and make promises to keep the rules of the Khalsa. He is waiting for the five members of the Khalsa who will represent the Panje Piare (the five beloved ones), but they are late. Then a phone call is received. The five men cannot make it today. They have been held up. What should those waiting do now?

- The class should discuss this situation in pairs or threes.

> **Questions to prompt discussion**
>
> - Would it matter if the Sikh was unable to perform the *ritual* of amrit? Why? Why not?
> - How do you think he would feel about not being able to do the *ritual*?
> - What difference would it make to him?
> - Which do you think might be the most important part of the *ritual* for a Sikh?
> - Why do you think that?
> - Are there any parts of the *ritual* that you think could be left out?
> - Which are they? Why have you thought of those particular parts?

- Duplicate and distribute the image provided (see CD artwork 13). Pupils complete the speech bubble for the Sikh, 'The *ritual* of amrit is important to me because ....'

Now go to Steps 4 and 5 in the book (pages 86–87) to complete the cycle of learning.

Resources on the CD

Figures

6.2   Cards – routines/rituals?
6.3   Writing frame – *A ritual is something that ...*
6.4   Debate about rituals

Artwork

1.   Chalice and paten
2.   This ritual is important to me because (Christian)
3.   Items found in a Buddhist temple
4.   The rituals of puja are important to me because (Buddhist)
5.   Arti lamp
6.   Arti ceremony
7.   The rituals of arti are important to me because (Hindu)
8.   Muslims performing ritual prayers
9.   The rituals of salah are important to me because (Muslim)
10.   A Jewish boy laying the tefillin
11.   The rituals of tefillin are important to me because (Jewish)
12.   A Sikh performing the amrit ritual
13.   The rituals of amrit are important to me because (Sikh)

Ritual: Christian

The Last Supper

Ritual: Buddhist

Buddhist puja
The arti ceremony

Ritual: Muslim

The Muslim ritual prayer, salah

Ritual: Jewish

The ritual of laying the tefillin

Ritual: Sikh

The amrit ritual

Various concepts

In this section there are six units of work, and every unit identifies a concept that has been selected because it is of central importance to the religion in which it is contextualised. Each unit explores one religion. In the book the concept *sacrifice* is contextualised through the Easter story. Pupils enquire into the concept as an example of the Christian belief that Jesus sacrificed his own life for humankind. The units of work from some of the major world faiths are listed below:

The concept of *suffering* in Buddhism
The concept of *devotion* in Hinduism
The concept of *freedom* in Judaism
The concept of *revelation* in Islam
The concept of *service* in Sikhism

The concept of *sacrifice* in Christianity

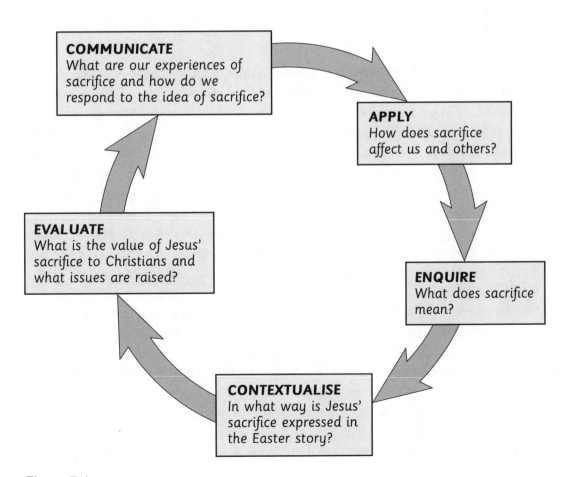

Figure 7.1

Step 1 Enquire

What does sacrifice mean?

- In small groups pupils produce a mind map or brainstorm around the word *sacrifice*. Compare and collate the ideas of the different groups.
- Watch the excerpt from the film of *The Lion, the Witch and the Wardrobe* about Aslan's sacrifice. What did Aslan do? Why? Discuss whether this helps pupils to describe the meaning of *sacrifice*.

Questions to prompt discussion

- What *sacrifice* did Aslan make? Why?
- What is a *sacrifice*?
- Can some *sacrifices* be bigger than others? Why? Why not?
- What is the biggest *sacrifice* anyone could make, do you think?

- Pupils devise a role-play scenario to illustrate *sacrifice*. Groups of pupils role play to others in the class in turn. What do class members think about the *sacrifice*? Is it a large or small *sacrifice*?

Step 2 Contextualise

In what way is Jesus's *sacrifice* expressed in the Easter story?

- Tell the class the Easter story (see below and on CD).

Jesus's sacrifice

Jesus and his followers had a meal together and Jesus told them how pleased he was to share the meal with them, before he had to suffer. After the meal they went to the Mount of Olives where he told his friends to pray. He moved some distance from them and fell to his knees to pray to God on his own. 'Father,' he said 'if you will, please take this suffering away from me.'

When he returned to the others, a crowd arrived, led by one of Jesus's followers called Judas. Some of the crowd carried swords and clubs. They arrested Jesus and took him away to the house of the Jewish high priest to be questioned. While Jesus was under arrest the men who were guarding him ridiculed him and beat him.

The chief Jewish priests, the elders and the teachers of the Jewish law formed a council. In the morning they met together to question Jesus and they asked him about what he had been saying to the crowds that listened to him. They believed that he had broken the sacred Jewish laws by claiming to be the son of God.

The Jewish council then took Jesus to Pilate who was the Roman governor. The Romans had control over the country and the governor had to decide on the punishment for criminals. The members of the Jewish council told Pilate that Jesus had been stirring up trouble and causing riots among the people. Pilate questioned Jesus closely and then spoke to the members of the Jewish council again. 'This man has not committed any of the crimes that you accuse him of.' he announced. Then he spoke to the crowds that had gathered outside. 'What shall I do with this man?' he asked the crowd. 'Crucify him! Crucify him!' they all shouted back. With that response Pilate sentenced Jesus to die on a cross.

Roman soldiers led Jesus away and he was tortured. The soldiers made a crown of thorns and put it on Jesus's head, they beat him and hit him over the head with a stick and they spat on him. Then Jesus was led to the site for crucifixions. He was nailed to a cross and hung there for hours. Just before he died Jesus shouted out 'My God, my God, why did you abandon me?' and then his breath left him.

Three days later Jesus appeared to his followers. They were all astounded to see Jesus again. Then he spoke to them about what was written in the Jewish laws and other Jewish writings. 'This is what is written,' he said. 'The Messiah must suffer and must rise from death three days later. The message about forgiveness of sins must be preached to everyone. I will be with you always to the end of the age.'

Questions to prompt discussion

- What was Jesus's *sacrifice* in this story?
- What do you think Christians believe the *sacrifice* was for?
- Are there any similarities between Jesus's *sacrifice* and Aslan's *sacrifice*?

- Pupils look at works of art representing aspects of Jesus's sacrifice (see artwork 1–4 on CD). The pupils should look closely at the images in groups. They should annotate them and use their notes to form a poem, or write 'art gallery' labels to go with each picture, explaining how each one expresses the idea of *sacrifice*.

Step 3 Evaluate

What is the value of Jesus's *sacrifice* to Christians and what issues are raised?

- Invite a Christian into class to answer pupils' questions on their beliefs about Jesus's sacrifice.
- Have a class discussion about Jesus's *sacrifice*.

Questions to prompt discussion

- Was Jesus's *sacrifice* worthwhile for Christians?
- Has it made any difference?
- What difference has it made to Christians?
- How do Christians feel about the *sacrifice* Jesus made as described in the story?

- Have a class debate on either the motion that
  'Jesus did not need to sacrifice himself' or the motion that
  'The sacrifice Jesus made was worthwhile.'
  Pupils prepare to talk either in favour of or against the chosen motion on the sheet provided (see Figure 7.2 on CD and below).

The motion
is _____

Points in favour	Points against

Figure 7.2

Step 4 Communicate

What are our experiences of *sacrifice* and how do we respond to the idea of *sacrifice*?

● Pupils consider and then talk in pairs about any *sacrifice* they have made or know that others have made. (Note: these can be simple *sacrifices*, like visiting Granddad in hospital instead of going to a friend's house to play computer games, or giving your last sausage to your baby brother when you want it yourself.) Compare and collate the ideas of the class.

Questions to prompt discussion

● What does *sacrifice* mean to you?
● Can you think of a time when you gave up something for someone?
● Have you ever made a *sacrifice* for a good cause? What was that?
● Do you know of anyone else who has made a *sacrifice* for someone else or for a good cause?

- Pupils draw or write about a *sacrifice* that someone has made or they have made themselves.
- Pupils role play the incidents they have discussed.

Step 5 Apply

How does *sacrifice* affect us and others?

- Pupils share their stories of *sacrifice* and discuss them.

Questions to prompt discussion

- Has your *sacrifice* made any difference to you or the other person or the cause? What difference?
- What is the motivation behind *sacrifice*?
- Can *sacrifice* ever be selfish or is it always for the good of someone else? (For instance, could someone make a *sacrifice* just to make themselves feel good?)
- Can a *sacrifice* ever have a bad effect?
- Is making a *sacrifice* always worth it?
- What does this discussion make you think about the Christian belief in the *sacrifice* Jesus made?

The concept of *suffering* in Buddhism

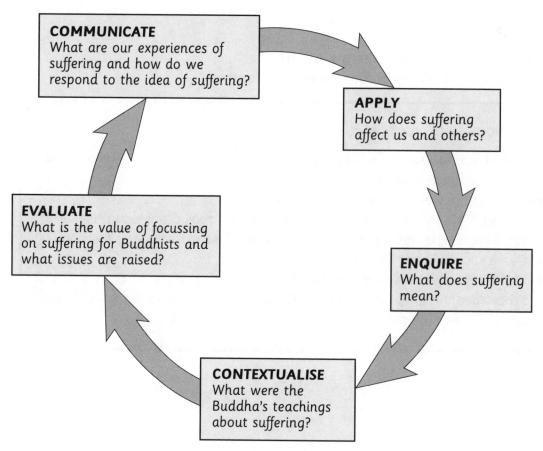

COMMUNICATE
What are our experiences of suffering and how do we respond to the idea of suffering?

APPLY
How does suffering affect us and others?

EVALUATE
What is the value of focussing on suffering for Buddhists and what issues are raised?

ENQUIRE
What does suffering mean?

CONTEXTUALISE
What were the Buddha's teachings about suffering?

Figure 7.3

Step 1 Enquire

What does *suffering* mean?

- Tell pupils the story of the woman and the mustard seed (see below and CD) and discuss with the class why the woman *suffered*.

> **Questions to prompt discussion**
>
> - Does everyone *suffer*?
> - What is *suffering*?
> - Are there different sorts of *suffering*?
> - Is some *suffering* worse than others?
> - Can two people have the same experience, but one person's *suffering* is worse than the other's? Why might that be?
> - Are there different degrees of *suffering*? Why? Why not?
> - Can you think of examples of different degrees of *suffering*?

A Buddhist story of suffering

There was once a woman called Kisagotami who had a son. Kisagotami's boy was playing by the river when he was bitten by a venomous snake. The poor boy died. Kisagotami was beside herself with grief. She swept the boy up in her arms and rushed him to where the Buddha, the great teacher, was teaching some of his followers.

She pushed past all the people and placed the dead boy in front of the Buddha. 'Oh Buddha, please, please bring my boy back to life if you can,' she pleaded. 'I have tried everyone in the village, but no one can help me.'

The Buddha was filled with compassion for the poor woman in her suffering. 'I will help you,' he said 'but first you must go to every house in the city. Bring me back a mustard seed from each house that has not been visited by death.'

Kisagotami rushed off to the city and knocked on door after door to collect mustard seeds as requested. But she collected none. At every single house she was told sad stories about loved ones who had died. The people in every house in the whole city had suffered in the same way that she had. Kisagotami began to realise why the Buddha had sent her on this mission. She could see that suffering and loss is part of everyone's life, and she was comforted by the knowledge that she was not alone in her sadness.

Kisagotami returned to the Buddha. 'Did you collect any mustard seeds?' he asked. 'No,' she replied, 'but I now know that nothing in life stays the same, and that death comes to everything.' Kisagotami became a Buddhist nun and followed the Buddha's teachings.

- Pupils in pairs or groups should share their ideas and note situations or experiences in the world and in life which could be described as *suffering*.
- Pupils in pairs write a definition or description of *suffering.*

Step 2 Contextualise

What were the Buddha's teachings about *suffering*?
- Show an image (see CD artwork 5) of Buddhists in calm meditation. Pupils speculate about what they might be doing that has any connection with *suffering.* Pupils discuss this in pairs then feed back in class discussion.
- Pupils should examine Buddha's teachings about *suffering* (dukkha) through the Four Noble Truths and the Eightfold Path (see Figure 7.3a below and CD).

The Four Noble Truths

1 Life is unsatisfactory. Life never runs smoothly. Everything changes all the time and we feel restless and dissatisfied when we cannot hang on to good experiences. This is *suffering*, and is called dukkha.
2 Dukkha arises. Humans have a basic desire to seek wellbeing, and this can be linked to greed, hatred and ignorance.
3 Dukkha can cease. A person must follow a certain lifestyle and stick to certain codes of behaviour in order to be free of dukkha.
4 The Eightfold Path is the Way. There are eight 'right' or 'appropriate' ways of behaving.

The Eightfold Path

1 Right understanding (see that life is unsatisfactory and nothing in life is permanent).
2 Right thought (recognise the power of the mind and that it should be filled with positive thoughts of kindness and compassion).
3 Right speech (avoid gossip or telling lies or speaking unkindly).
4 Right action (do not kill, steal or behave immorally sexually).
5 Right livelihood (have a job which does not hurt anyone or destroy life).
6 Right effort (think carefully about what you say or do).
7 Right awareness (concentrate on what you do and be alert).
8 Right concentration (be attentive to keep peaceful and calm).

- Pupils in groups should use drama and story telling to express situations in relation to the Eightfold Path. Other pupils guess which aspect of the Eightfold Path each group is expressing.
- Invite a Buddhist monk or nun or a lay Buddhist to speak to the pupils about dukkha.
- Pupils should write a letter from the Buddha to his disciples explaining to them how dukkha affects their lives, and how to cope with dukkha.

Step 3 Evaluate

What is the value of focusing on *suffering* for Buddhists, and what issues are raised?

- Discuss with pupils how Buddhists feel about *suffering* (dukkha).

Questions to prompt discussion

- Do Buddhists feel differently about situations of *suffering* from non-Buddhists, do you think? Why? Why not?
- How do Buddhists respond to *suffering* (dukkha)?
- Is this always easy?
- Would two Buddhists faced with the same situation always respond in the same way? Why? Why not?
- Do you think the Eightfold Path is helpful for Buddhists?

- Arrange a class debate on the motion *'The Buddha's Eightfold Path is not relevant in our society.'* Pupils speak for or against the motion. They should make notes in 'for' and 'against' columns (see Figure 7.2 on page 102 and on CD).

Step 4 Communicate

What are our experiences of *suffering* and how do we respond to the idea of *suffering*?

- Pupils discuss in pairs examples of *suffering* in their own lives and their own response to these situations. (Note that pupils should not feel they must share traumatic experiences. They should be encouraged to consider their experiences in terms of the Buddhist view of their 'unsatisfactory' nature.)
- Pupils role play different situations of *suffering* in groups.
- Pupils paint a picture or write a poem or create some simple sounds to express their experiences of *suffering* (unsatisfactory experiences).

Step 5 Apply

How does *suffering* affect us and others?

- Continuing from the session described above, when pupils present their pictures, music or poems, other members of the class can discuss a range of possible responses to situations of *suffering*.

Questions to prompt discussion

- Does everyone *suffer*? Why? Why not?
- How does *suffering* affect people?
- Is there a way to relieve *suffering*?
- What could that be?
- Can *suffering* ever be a good thing? In what ways?
- Has learning about the Buddha's view of *suffering* changed the way you think about *suffering*? Why? Why not? In what ways?

The concept of *devotion* in Hinduism

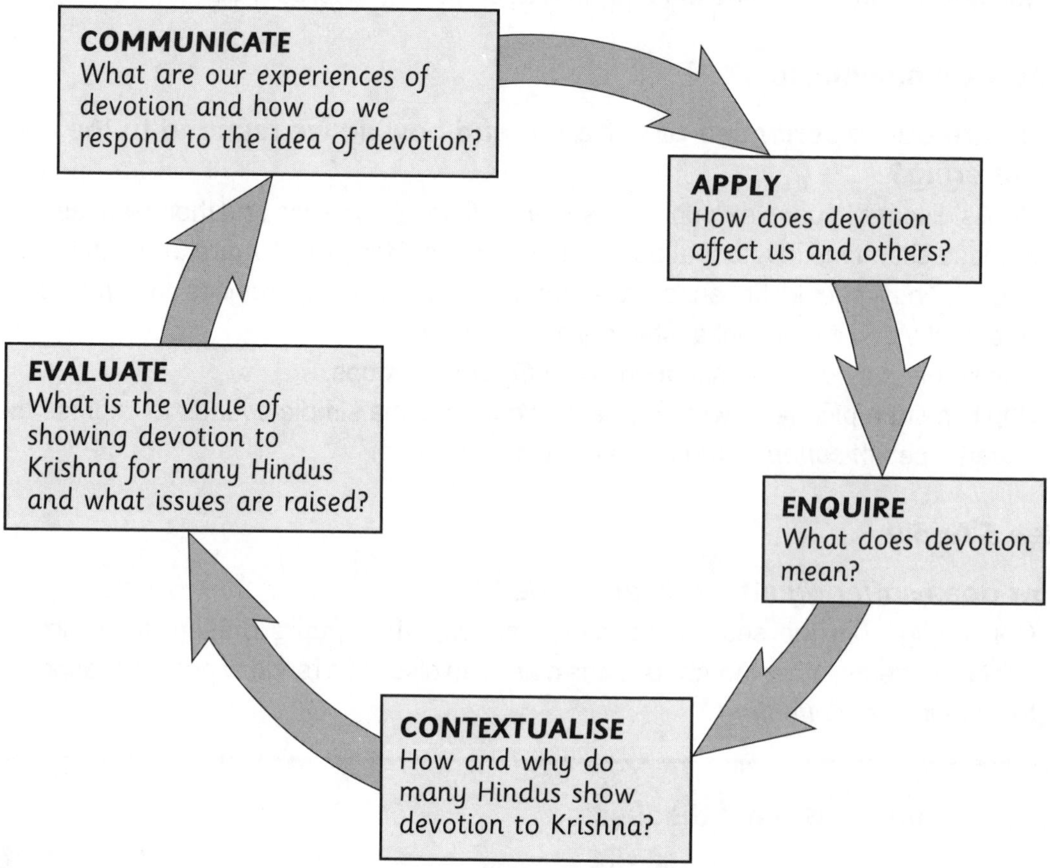

COMMUNICATE
What are our experiences of devotion and how do we respond to the idea of devotion?

APPLY
How does devotion affect us and others?

ENQUIRE
What does devotion mean?

CONTEXTUALISE
How and why do many Hindus show devotion to Krishna?

EVALUATE
What is the value of showing devotion to Krishna for many Hindus and what issues are raised?

Figure 7.4

Step 1 Communicate

What are our experiences of *devotion* and how do we respond to the idea of *devotion*?

- Pupils in pairs consider people who appear *devoted* to someone (for instance, Batman and Robin, the Queen and Prince Philip or Great Britain, a farmer and a sheepdog). Can they list people who are *devoted* to other people or animals? Collate and discuss their ideas as a class.
- Pupils now consider who they are *devoted* to, or who is *devoted* to them, discuss this in groups of two or three and then as a class.
- Pupils draw pictures and annotate them: 'I am devoted to … because …' or '… is devoted to me because ….'

> **Questions to prompt discussion**
>
> - Who are you *devoted* to? Why?
> - Is anyone *devoted* to an animal?
> - Can a person be *devoted* to someone when that *devotion* is not returned?
> - Why are you *devoted* to a person or animal?
> - How do you show your *devotion* or how do others show it to you?

Step 2 **Apply**

How does *devotion* affect us and others?

- Distribute the questions provided (on CD and Figure 7.5). The pupils in pairs take 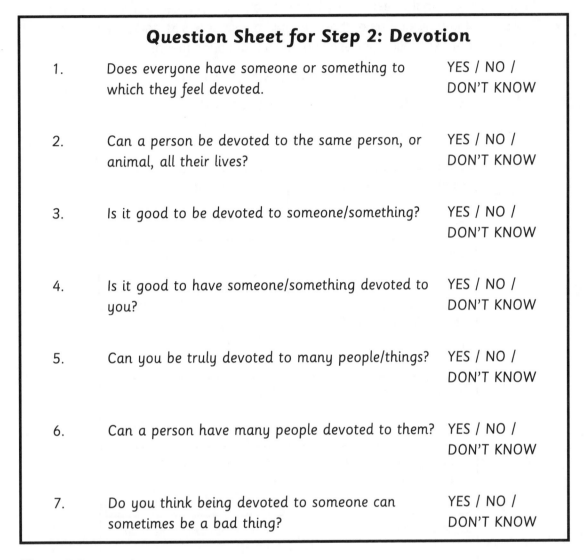 turns to ask each other the questions and record the answers.
- Count up and collate the answers on a whiteboard.
- The class should discuss the results. Are there any surprises? Why? Why not?

Question Sheet for Step 2: Devotion

1.	Does everyone have someone or something to which they feel devoted.	YES / NO / DON'T KNOW
2.	Can a person be devoted to the same person, or animal, all their lives?	YES / NO / DON'T KNOW
3.	Is it good to be devoted to someone/something?	YES / NO / DON'T KNOW
4.	Is it good to have someone/something devoted to you?	YES / NO / DON'T KNOW
5.	Can you be truly devoted to many people/things?	YES / NO / DON'T KNOW
6.	Can a person have many people devoted to them?	YES / NO / DON'T KNOW
7.	Do you think being devoted to someone can sometimes be a bad thing?	YES / NO / DON'T KNOW

Figure 7.5

Questions to prompt discussion

- How does it feel to have someone (a person or animal) *devoted* to you?
- Could there be times when someone being *devoted* to you is not good? Why? When?
- How do you feel if you are *devoted* to someone (a person or animal)?
- How do you show your *devotion*?
- In what situations might you lose that feeling of *devotion*?
- Is showing *devotion* always a good thing? Why? Why not?

Step 3 Enquire

What does *devotion* mean?

- Pupils work in threes. The teacher should make a set of cards for each group (see CD Figure 7.6). Each group should discuss and select what they think are the eight most important ways of showing *devotion.* They should be prepared to give reasons for their choices.
- Pupils discuss with the rest of the class their choice of cards, and give reasons.
- Pupils, back in their groups of three, should consider words and phrases that would contribute to a description or definition of what *devotion* means.

Activity Sheet – Step 3: DEVOTION

How should people show devotion to others?

Select 8 cards that you think are most important.

Think about them a lot	Provide all their food
Give them presents	Be with them as much as possible
Talk to them as much as you can	Make sure they are pleased with you
Do whatever they want	Praise them a lot
Talk to them when you need their help	Help them when they need help
Give and take	Think about them on their birthdays
Tell them how much you like them	Ignore them

Figure 7.6

Step 4 Contextualise

How and why do many Hindus show *devotion* to Krishna?

- Show the class a picture of a Hindu showing *devotion* at the shrine of Krishna (see CD artwork 6). Pupils should identify and describe the activities observed.
- Making reference to the cards used in Step 3, ask the class, which of the statements on the cards can be applied to a Hindu at the shrine of Krishna?
- The class should discuss their responses and ideas.

- Pupils should produce a simple illustrated guide book for a Hindu child on 'How to show devotion to Krishna'.
- Ask pupils to study the image of Krishna (see CD artwork 7).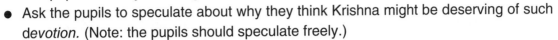
- Ask the pupils to speculate about why they think Krishna might be deserving of such de*votion*. (Note: the pupils should speculate freely.)
- Investigate some stories about Krishna. This could be teacher-led or different groups of pupils could investigate different stories (see below and CD and the section about the concept of God in Hinduism in this book) (pages 39–41).

Krishna and his great powers

When Krishna was very young he went to the river with his friends, the cowherd boys, and the calves they were looking after. They stopped on the river bank to have a picnic and to rest while the calves drank the cool water.

They were having such a good time that they failed to notice that the calves had wandered off. When the boys eventually noticed they were very worried about them. What if the calves were in danger?

'Don't worry,' Krishna reassured them. 'I will go and look for them and bring them all back.'

Krishna set off, looking high and low for the lost calves, but could not find them anywhere. However, Krishna was not alone. Brahma, a powerful God, was watching Krishna searching. Krishna looked like an ordinary boy, so how could he be the great, Supreme Being that people talked of, he wondered? Brahma decided to put Krishna's powers to the test.

Brahma had the power to send all the cowherd boys and all the calves to sleep, and he placed them safely in a cave where they would not be found.

Krishna failed to find the calves, and returned to the river bank. The cowherd boys were missing too, and he realised that Brahma was the culprit. But what was he to do about the missing boys and calves? He decided to use his amazing powers, and he turned himself into each of the boys and each of the calves. He made himself into identical copies of each boy and each animal and they all returned to the village.

How pleased were all the mothers to see their boys back safely, and how they hugged them. How pleased were all the cows to see their calves back safely, and how they licked them.

Life carried on the village as before, and many months later the great God Brahma came to see what was happening. He was amazed. All the boys and all the calves seemed to be playing happily with Krishna as before, yet Brahma was sure that he had sent them to sleep and hidden them in a cave. He was immensely puzzled.

Krishna decided to reveal what had happened, and turned each of the copies of the boys and the calves into the great Supreme Being Lord Vishnu. Each being had many arms, wore a fantastic gold headdress and yellow garments, and was adorned with jewellery. A great light shone from them. Brahma felt ashamed about his trick and hid his eyes from the light. 'I now know that you are the Supreme Being,' said Brahma. 'You are the Master and you are full of knowledge and full of bliss.' he added.

Krishna then made the forms of Vishnu disappear. and returned the sleeping boys and the calves to the river bank and woke them. When the boys saw Krishna they were very pleased. 'Well done, Krishna,' they said. 'You have found the calves, and you have only been gone a minute.'

- Pupils should list Krishna's attributes and powers identified in the stories.
- Pupils should produce artwork of Krishna showing his attributes and powers. Create a display of the pupils' work.

Step 5 Evaluate

What is the value of showing *devotion* to Krishna for many Hindus, and what issues are raised?

- Ask pupils to imagine a situation in which members of the Hindu temple read a newspaper report (see below and CD Figure 7.7).
- Divide the pupils into groups, with some pupils in role as government officials and others as members of the Hindu community. In their groups they should prepare notes for a meeting between both parties.
- Hold the meeting. How might each group argue its case?
- The pupils should write a letter from a Hindu to the government organisation DORCS, explaining the value and importance of showing *devotion*.
- Discuss with the class: having explored their own responses to *devotion* and how it impacts on their lives and others' lives, what do they think about Hindus showing *devotion*?

Plans to Scrap Showy Forms of Worship

A spokesperson for the government watchdog organisation DORCS (Department Overseeing Religious Communities and Societies) said today that any outward show of religious devotion is to be banned shortly. He said that members of religious groups should restrict their worship to silent prayer and should remain motionless throughout worship. He said "Outward shows of devotion can incite racial hatred from those outside the religious group".

Figure 7.7

Questions to prompt discussion

- Do you think it is important for Hindus to be *devoted* to Krishna (or other deities)? Why? Why not?
- Why do you think they need to show their *devotion*?
- How does it affect them, do you think?
- If they didn't show *devotion*, would it matter? Why? Why not?
- If they didn't feel *devoted* to Krishna, or another deity, would that matter? Why? Why not?

The concept of *freedom* in Judaism

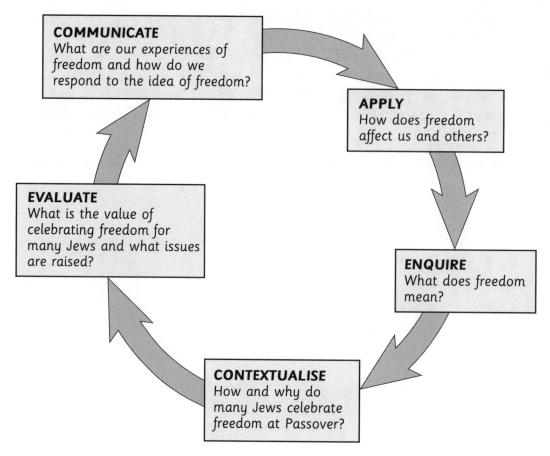

Figure 7.8

Step 1 Enquire

What does *freedom* mean?

- In groups of two or three, the pupils should brainstorm the concept of *freedom* or produce concept maps for the concept *freedom*.
- The groups should pair up and compare their responses. They can highlight the common ideas and also identify differences.
- The teacher should collate the different groups' ideas, on the whiteboard.
- Pupils produce simple poems or verses on the theme 'Freedom is ....'

> #### Questions to prompt discussion:
>
> - Is *freedom* a good thing? Why? Why not?
> - Would *freedom* be good if you were three years old?
> - Is there such a thing as complete *freedom*?
> - What would that be like?
> - Does anyone have complete *freedom*?
> - Could *freedom* be a negative idea? Why? When?

Step 2 **Contextualise**

How and why do many Jews celebrate *freedom* at Passover?

- The teacher should show the class a picture of a Jewish family celebrating freedom at the seder meal at Passover (Pesach) (see CD artwork 8) and pupils should speculate on possible connections to *freedom.*
- Role play a simplified version of a seder meal with the pupils (see CD and below for information). Focus attention on the story (see page 43 on the Jewish concept of God) of God leading the Jews to freedom from slavery in Egypt. Draw pupils' attention to the symbolic food and traditions that are reminders of *freedom.*
- Act out the Exodus story with the class. Pupils show the contrast between slavery and *freedom* in their movements and facial expressions.
- Pupils should produce some reflective writing or diary entries from a Jew in slavery in Egypt and then free in the desert.

The seder meal: a celebration of freedom

For this special family meal the table is laid beautifully with the best crockery that is only used for Passover. There are two candlesticks on the table.

A plate with symbolic food is placed on the table. On the plate is:

- a lamb bone (representing the Passover lamb which was killed and its blood painted over the doors of Jewish houses)
- parsley (which is dipped in the salt water and eaten as a reminder of the Jewish tears that were shed when they were slaves in Egypt)
- bitter herbs such as horseradish (as a reminder of the bitterness of slavery)
- a roasted egg (a reminder of new life and hope for freedom)
- haroset, which is a mixture of chopped nuts, apples and wine (as a reminder of the mortar that was used by the Jewish slaves when they were building in Egypt)

There is also a small bowl of salt water or vinegar.

There are three matzos, which are wafer-thin hard biscuits. These are reminders of the hardship of slavery and the way the Jews had to leave Egypt in a hurry.

Each member of the family has a wine glass, and there is a spare place set with a special glass, which is referred to as Elijah's cup.

Seder means 'order'. The way that Jewish families celebrate freedom at the *seder* meal follows the same 'order' every year. This is true of Jews all over the world.

1. The mother lights the two candles and says a special prayer to mark the start of the meal.
2. Traditionally, the youngest of the family asks four questions:
   - Why is this night different from all other nights? Why do we eat matzos tonight?
   - Why do we eat bitter herbs at Pesach?
   - Why do we sip twice?
   - Why do we lean back at the table?
3. The father tells the story of the Jews leaving Egypt where they were slaves, to find freedom in the desert.

During the meal four cups of wine are drunk. Each cup reminds the Jews of the promises that God made to them:
'I will free you from Egypt.'
'I will free you from slavery.'
'I will lead you home.'
'You are my people.'

5   During the seder someone in the family opens the front door to look for Elijah. A Jewish tradition says that Elijah will come one day and there will be *freedom* for everyone and the world will be at peace.

6   At the end of the meal everyone says together 'Next Year Jerusalem'. Jerusalem is regarded by Jews as the land that was promised to them by God.

Step 3 Evaluate

What is the value of celebrating *freedom* for many Jews, and what issues are raised?

- Duplicate the statements in Figure 7.9 and on CD and cut them up to provide sets of cards for pupils working in pairs. Pupils put them into an order of priority based on how they think a Jewish 10-year-old might order them.
- Each pair of pupils should swap places with another pair and see their order of priorities. Are there any similarities or differences that they notice? The pupils should discuss and justify the reasons for their order.
- The teacher should ask if there are any issues or questions raised, and discuss them with the class.
- Arrange for a Jewish visitor to come to the class, Pupils should prepare questions for the visitor around the issue of *freedom*.
- The pupils should complete a speech bubble for someone Jewish, 'Celebrating freedom is important to me because ....'

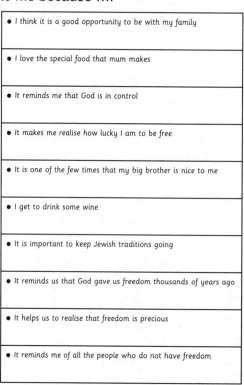

• I think it is a good opportunity to be with my family
• I love the special food that mum makes
• It reminds me that God is in control
• It makes me realise how lucky I am to be free
• It is one of the few times that my big brother is nice to me
• I get to drink some wine
• It is important to keep Jewish traditions going
• It reminds us that God gave us freedom thousands of years ago
• It helps us to realise that freedom is precious
• It reminds me of all the people who do not have freedom

Figure 7.9 What is the value of celebrating freedom at Passover?

Step 4 Communicate

What are our experiences of *freedom* and how do we respond to the idea of *freedom*?

- The pupils should consider and list words and ideas that express the opposite of being free (for instance, being restricted, trapped, held down, held back, stopped, prevented). Compare and collate their ideas.
- Ask the pupils to consider times when they have experienced these feelings, and share this information with a partner. Compare and discuss a few of these ideas with the class.
- Pupils in pairs should decide on body language that illustrates the feeling of lacking *freedom* – freeze frame. Half the class should demonstrate their freeze frame while the other half watch and comment, then the two groups should swap roles.
- Now pupils should discuss the feeling when the restriction is removed. How does *freedom* feel? In pairs, the pupils should discuss examples, then each should create another position to express the feeling of *freedom.* The pupils should freeze frame as above.
- What do pupils like to do when they have *freedom*? Discuss this as a class.
- Pupils should complete a writing frame, 'I felt free when ....'

Step 5 Apply

How does *freedom* affect us and others?

- Have a class discussion using the prompts below.

Questions to prompt discussions

- Is *freedom* important to you? Why? Why not?
- Do you want *freedom* all the time? Why? Why not?
- Who stops or restricts your *freedom*?
- Is *freedom* more important as you get older? Why? Why not?
- Do you think you will ever have total *freedom*?
- Would you want total *freedom*?
- Do you want *freedom* on particular occasions?
- If you had total *freedom*, what would you do?

- Have a simple class debate about freedom. The motion is *'Everyone should have freedom.'* The pupils should prepare points to make, then speak in favour of or against the motion.

The concept of *revelation* in Islam

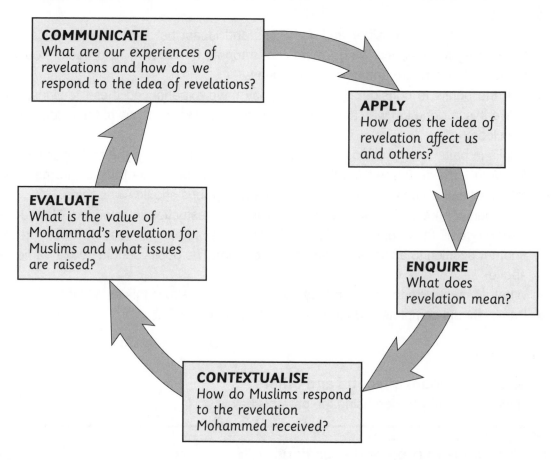

COMMUNICATE
What are our experiences of revelations and how do we respond to the idea of revelations?

APPLY
How does the idea of revelation affect us and others?

EVALUATE
What is the value of Mohammad's revelation for Muslims and what issues are raised?

ENQUIRE
What does revelation mean?

CONTEXTUALISE
How do Muslims respond to the revelation Mohammed received?

Figure 7.10

Step 1 Enquire

What does *revelation* mean?

 ● Tell the class the story of Muhammad's revelation on Mount Hira (see below and CD).

The *revelation Muhammad received*

Muhammad (pbuh) was a wonderful human being. He was fair and calm and honest and good, and had great compassion for people. However, he was often troubled by the world. He could see that there was often lying and cheating, arguments and aggression, and this upset Muhammad. When he was troubled he would escape to quiet places and be alone to meditate and to pray and to puzzle over the mysteries in life.

One of the places where Muhammad liked to spend time was a cave on a mountain called Hira. It was in the cave of Hira where Muhammad had a most amazing experience. One day his deep thoughts were suddenly disturbed by a bright light which caught his eye. He slowly looked up, and in the blinding light was the form of an angel. 'Recite,' called the figure in the light. 'But what shall I say? I don't know what to say!' stuttered Muhammad in his fear and amazement. 'Recite,' ordered the angel. Suddenly Muhammad knew what to recite. Truth had been revealed to him. It was as if the words were written on his heart, and they tumbled out of his mouth.

The angel left as suddenly as it had arrived, and Muhammad was left filled with doubt and confusion.

He raced down the mountain to tell Khadijah, his wife about the experience. 'Be calm, Muhammad,' she whispered. 'A message from Allah has been revealed to you .Take heart. You have been chosen.'

Muhammad knew how powerful this revelation was. His searching for truth had been answered, and he had a revelation from Allah to reveal to all the people.

Muhammad had many more revelations, and he memorised all that he had been told. Muhammad shared all these messages with the people. He recited the messages everywhere he went, and he gathered many loyal followers who remembered and recorded the messages for all to hear. More and more people heard the words revealed from Allah, and their lives were changed.

Now these messages from Allah are recorded in the Holy Qur'an and today, Muslims all over the world learn to recite the holy words, as Muhammad had done, all those years ago.

Questions to prompt discussion

- What do you think is the most important part of the story? Why?
- What do you think is the point of the story?
- The story talks about a *revelation* from Allah given to Muhammad. What do you think *revelation* means?
- What words and phrases can you think of that would help explain the meaning of the word *revelation* to others?

- The pupils should contribute ideas to a class definition or description of the concept of *revelation*.

Step 2 Contextualise

How do Muslims respond to the *revelation* Muhammad received?

- Show the class a picture of Muslim children studying the Qur'an (see CD artwork 9).
- Pupils should speculate about what they can see and what it has to do with Allah's *revelation* to Muhammad.
- Pupils should research on websites or in books or other resources how Muslims treat and use the Qur'an which contains *revelations* from Allah.
- Share with the class the information (supplied below and on CD) about the Qur'an.

The Qur'an

- Muhammad (pbuh) learned to recite, off by heart, all the *revelations* given to him by Allah.
- Many of Muhammad's followers listened to the *revelations* from Muhammad and also learned to recite them
- The *revelations* from Allah were written down by Muhammad's followers after his death. These writings formed the Qur'an.
- Every copy of the Qur'an is identical and is written in Arabic.
- Muslims learn to read Arabic so that they can read and learn to recite parts of the Qur'an.
- Some Muslims learn to recite the whole Qur'an as Muhammad did.
- The Qur'an is treated with great respect. It is placed on a stand when it is being studied. Often, hands are washed before the book is handled. When it is not in use it is kept wrapped and often placed on a high shelf above the height of other books.
- The *revelations* from Allah include:

Show kindness to your parents and to near relatives, orphans, those in need, the neighbour who is related to you as well as the neighbour who is a stranger and your companion by your side and the wayfarer and anyone who is your responsibility.

You who believe, whenever you intend to pray, wash your faces and your hands up to the elbows, and wash your head and wash your feet up to the ankles.

Children of Adam, wear your best clothes at every time of worship.

You who believe, liquor and gambling, idols and raffles, are only a work of Satan; avoid them that you may prosper.

- Pupils should create a simple conversation between a Muslim child and her mother. The child asks about the Qur'an and the mother explains why it is treated with such care. This can be recorded by pupils working with partners.

Step 3 Evaluate

What is the value of Muhammad's *revelation* for Muslims, and what issues are raised?

- Pupils should be arranged in small groups. Pupils take it in turn to be in the 'hot seat' in role as a Muslim and to answer the other pupils' questions about the value of the *revelations* in the Qur'an to them.
- Invite a Muslim visitor to the class, to answer pupils' questions about the value of Allah's *revelation* to Muslims.

Step 4 Communicate

What are our experiences of *revelation* and how do we respond to the idea of *revelation*?

- The teacher should ask the pupils to think about other stories of 'revelations' (such as Archimedes in his bath, Newton and the apple that fell on his head, and the Buddha and his enlightenment).

> **Questions to prompt discussion**
>
> - Are these *revelations* or should we call them something else?
> - Is a *revelation* always associated with God, do you think?
> - Can people have *revelations* that have nothing to do with God?

- Pupils in pairs or threes should share incidents when they have had an 'Oh, I get it!' moment (when they have not understood something or not known about something, and then it has become clear, has become 'revealed' to them).
- Pupils share their ideas, describing incidents in terms of 'before the revelation' and 'after the revelation' (for instance, 'I didn't get fractions at first and kept feeling very confused, then suddenly it all made sense and I felt ....').
- The pupils draw and annotate their experiences and share them with the class.
- The class should discuss: do we think these are *revelations* or should we use another word?

Step 5 Apply

How does the idea of a *revelation* affect us and others?

- Discuss how *revelations* affect people using the prompts below.

> **Questions to prompt discussion**
>
> - How have your personal 'revelations' affected you?
> - Are there any *revelations* that you think have affected the world?
> - What are they? Where are they from?
> - How have *revelations* affected the world?
> - Are *revelations* always for the good of humankind, or can *revelations* be negative? How? Why?
> - If you heard on the news a report that someone had received a *revelation* from God, what would you think? Why?
> - Has enquiring into the idea of *revelation* changed the way you think about things in any way? How?

- The pupils should complete the writing frame provided (see below and CD Figure 7.11.)

How have revelations affected the world?

Figure 7.11

The concept of *service* in Sikhism

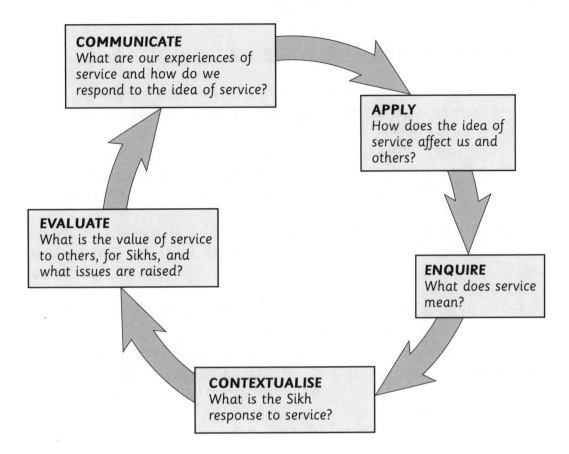

Figure 7.12

Step 1 Enquire

What does *service* mean?

● Provide copies of the words and phrases provided below and on CD Figure 7.13. The ◀
pupils should highlight the words and phrases that they associate with the concept of
service. Share their ideas in a class discussion.

● The pupils in pairs should think of any activities that they might describe as a *service*
to others. Collate and share their ideas in class discussion.

● As a class decide on a description or definition of *service.*

● Show picture of Sikhs serving others at the shared meal in the gurdwara (see CD ◀
artwork 10). What does the picture show that has anything to do with *service*? The
pupils should speculate and discuss.

> **When someone provides a service, what does that mean?**
>
> helping someone   taking their money   trying to please   gaining favour
>
> doing a duty   doing what you are paid for   human kindness
>
> doing as you are told   doing what is expected   supporting someone
>
> being a creep   putting others first   getting people to like you   doing a job

Figure 7.13

Step 2 Contextualise

What is the Sikh response to *service*?

▶ • Tell the pupils the story below (also see CD).

> ### *A good man who provided service to others*
>
> Years ago the Sikhs had been involved in a terrible battle. After the fighting stopped there were many soldiers left on the battlefield. Some were injured and exhausted, others were dying.
>
> A good man called Bhai Kanaiyaji went onto the battlefield to see if he could ease the suffering that he could see. He took water and gently helped the wounded and dying men sip from his water carrier. He spoke kindly to the soldiers and helped in any way he could.
>
> Some Sikh soldiers saw what Bhai Kanaiyaji was doing, and became furious. He was even helping the enemy soldiers! They rushed across the battlefield and grabbed Bhai Kanaiyaji and hurried him off to Guru Gobind Singh, their great Guru and the leader of the Sikhs.
>
> 'Bhai Kanaiyaji is helping everyone on the battlefield, he is also helping the enemy!' the soldiers complained. Bhai Kanaiyaji spoke calmly to Guru Gobind Singh, their leader. 'You have always said that all people should be treated equally as we are all children of God,' he said. 'You have taught us to give service to everyone who might need it. I did not see any enemies on the battlefield, but I saw all the men as my brothers.'
>
> Guru Gobind Singh was pleased with what he heard. 'You are a good man,' he said. 'I want more Sikhs to be like you.'

> ### Questions to prompt discussion
>
> • Why do you think this story is important to Sikhs?
> • What *service* did the good man provide?
> • Do you think he should have provided a *service* to his enemies? Why? Why not?
> • What does this story teach Sikhs about who is deserving of *service*?

• Distribute or show on an interactive whiteboard the image of Sikhs providing *service* at the Sikh gurdwara, and the supplied information below. (See the Service in Sikhism section on CD.)

Service in Sikhism

- Sikhs believe that *service* can be given to others in different ways:
- Intellectual *service* can be given through study and teaching others.
- Giving is a *service* which can be in the form of money or items given as charity.
- Physical work can be a *service* to others seen as giving of time and effort.
- *Service* given to others is called sewa (pronounced saiva) in Sikhism.
- Sikhs believe that *serving* others is a way in which they can feel closer to God.
- All Sikhs provide *service* to others. It does not matter if they are rich or poor, if they are important people in the community or if they are not.
- When Sikhs go to worship at the gurdwara different members of the community take it in turns to prepare a meal for all the people there, as a form of *service* to others. They also clean the building and perhaps polish the shoes of others.

- The pupils in pairs should draw a picture of a Sikh involved in a form of service to others, and annotate it: 'This Sikh is providing a service by ….'

Step 3 Evaluate

What is the value of *service* to others for Sikhs? What issues are raised?

- Duplicate and prepare sets of cards (see CD and Figure 7.14).
- Pupils in pairs or threes should put the cards in what they think a Sikh would see as their order of priority.
- Compare and discuss the order in which pairs or group of pupils organised their cards. Pupils should explain the reasons for the order of their cards.

Because they would get bored if they didn't	Because when they serve others they are serving God
Because they are doing as the Sikh Gurus told them to years ago	Because everyone is equal
Because everyone has a responsibility to look after other human beings	Because they want to please the other Sikhs
Because they won't get any food at the Gurdwara if they don't help	Because they love all their Sikh brothers and sisters

Figure 7.14 Why do Sikhs provide service (sewa) to others?

Questions to prompt discussion

- What did you have as the most important statement? Why?
- Do others agree or disagree? Why?
- What other statements did you have as a priority? Why?
- Were there any statements that you did not think were appropriate for a Sikh? What? Why?
- Do you think all Sikhs would agree with what you have as priorities? Why? Why not?

- Invite a Sikh to speak to the pupils about *service* (sewa) and answer pupils' questions.
- The class should visit a gurdwara if possible, to see and ask about how Sikhs provide *service* to others.

Step 4 Communicate

What are our experiences of *service* and how do we respond to the idea of *service*?

- Pupils should close their eyes and sit quietly and go through their day so far, mentally noting when someone has provided a *service* for them.
- Pupils compare their thoughts with partners, then share them as a class.
- Discuss the sorts of action they think could be described as a *service*.
- Now the pupils consider, in the same way, any *service* they have provided for anyone else. Compare with partners, then share them as a class.
- Now ask the pupils to consider their lifetimes.
  - Can they think of an incident where someone provided a service that was notable
  - Have they ever provided a service that they thought was notable
  - Do they know of any stories of people who have provided a service to others?
- Discuss and share ideas as a class.

Step 5 Apply

How does the idea of *service* affect us and others?
- Show the statements provided as Figure 7.15 (also on CD) on an interactive whiteboard, or by providing copies for pupils to read.
- The pupils should highlight or note the statements that they agree with most.

Why would you provide a service for others?

1. Because it gives me a warm glow inside

2. Because I want someone else to feel happy

3. Because I want to make friends

4. Because I want the person to do me a favour in return

5. Because I have been taught to think about others

6. Because there should be give and take in the world

7. Because other people need my help

8. Because I want to be accepted

9. Because I like the people I provide a service to

10. Because selfish people are often unpopular.

Figure 7.15

Questions to prompt discussion
- Which statement did you agree with most?
- Can you say why?
- Which did you disagree with most? Why?
- Do you think *service* to others can sometimes be selfish? Why? Why not?
- Does *service* always have a positive result?
- Can you think of a situation when someone providing a *service* might have a negative effect?
- Has the enquiry into *service* made you think differently about anything?

Resources on the CD

Figures

7.2   Class debate template
7.5   Question sheet – Devotion
7.6   Activity sheet – Devotion
7.7   Newspaper report
7.9   Statements – What is the value of celebrating freedom?
7.11 Writing frame – how have revelations affected the world?
7.13 When someone provides a service
7.14 Cards – Why do Sikhs proved service to others?
7.15 Why would you provide a service for others?

Artwork

1–4. Jesus's sacrifice
  5.   Buddhists in calm meditation
  6.   Hindu showing devotion at the shrine of Krishna
  7.   Image of Krishna
  8.   A Jewish family celebrating freedom
  9.   Muslim children studying the Qur'an
 10.   Sikhs serving others in the gurdwara

Stories: Christian

Jesus's sacrifice

Stories: Buddhist

A Buddhist story of suffering

Stories: Hindu

Krishna and his great powers

Stories: Muslim

Muhammad's revelation on Mount Hira

Stories: Sikh

A good man who provided service to others

Further information

The Four Noble Truths and the Eightfold Plan
The Seder meal: a celebration of freedom
The Qur'an
Service in Sikhism